Take It to Your Seat Centers

Reading & Language

4

Center	Skill	Page

Using the Centers

The centers in this book are intended for skill practice and reinforcement, not as an introduction to skills. It is important to model the use of each center before students are asked to do the tasks independently.

Why Use Centers?

- Centers are a motivating way for students to practice important skills.
- They appeal especially to kinesthetic and visual learners.
- The 12 centers in this book are self-contained and portable. Students can work at a desk, at a table, or on a rug.
- Once you've made the centers, they're ready to use at any time.

Before Using Centers

You and your students will enjoy using the centers more if you think through logistical considerations. Here are a few questions to resolve ahead of time:

- Will students select a center, or will you assign the centers and use them as a skill assessment tool?
- Will there be a specific block of time for centers, or will the centers be used throughout the day as students complete other work?
- Where will you place the centers for easy access by students?
- What procedure will students use when they need help with the center tasks?
- Will students use the answer key to check their own work?
- How will you use the center checklist to track student completion of the centers?

A Place for Centers

Make the centers ahead of time so that they are ready for student use whenever specific skill practice is indicated.

Store the prepared centers in a filing box or crate. If you wish the centers to be self-checking, include the answer key with the center materials.

Introducing the Centers

Use the student direction cover page to review the skill to be practiced.

Read each step to the students and model what to do, showing students the center pieces.

Record Progress

Use the center checklist (page 4) to record the date and student achievement.

Making the Centers

Included in Each Center

- Ⓐ Student direction cover page
- Ⓑ Task cards and/or mats
- Ⓒ Reproducible student response form
- Ⓓ Answer key

Materials Needed

- Colored file folders with inside pockets
- Small envelopes or plastic self-closing bags (for storing cut task cards)
- Pencils and marking pens (for labeling envelopes)
- Scissors
- Double-sided tape
- Laminated center pieces
- Answer key pages

Steps to Follow

1. Tape the student direction page to the front of the file folder.
2. Place the reproduced response forms in the left-hand pocket.
3. Laminate the task cards and mats. Put the cut cards in a labeled envelope or plastic self-closing bag. Place the mats and task cards in the right-hand pocket of the file folder.

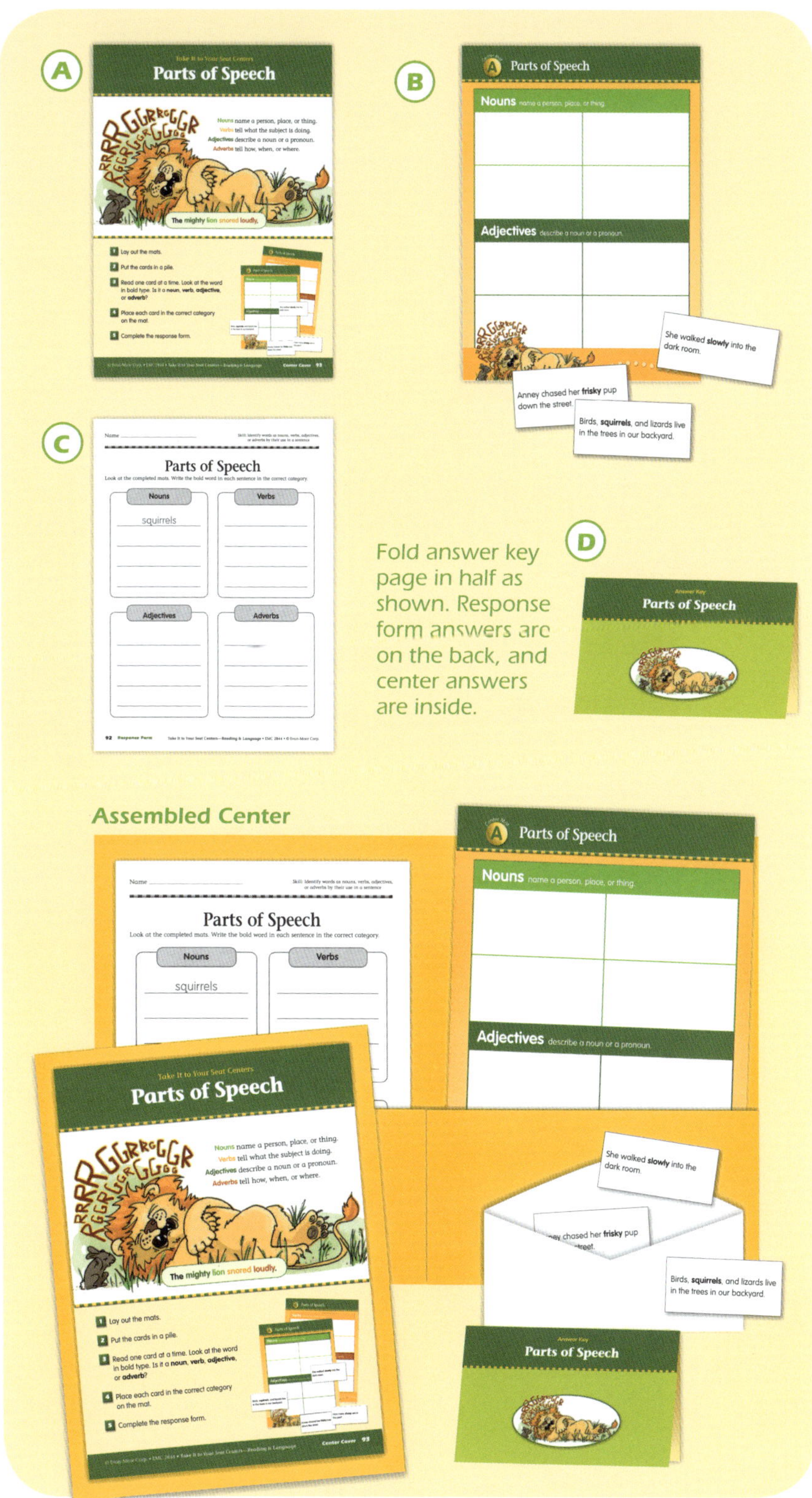

Student ______________________________

Center Checklist

Center / Skills	Skill Level	Date
1. Alphabetical Order Alphabetize words in a group to the fourth or fifth letter		
2. Synonyms/Antonyms Distinguish between synonyms as words with almost the same meanings and antonyms as words with opposite meanings		
3. Sequencing Use signal words to sequence a nonfiction passage and a "how to" passage		
4. Prefixes Form new words from a prefix and a base word, and demonstrate understanding of the meanings		
5. Suffixes Form new words from a base word and a suffix, and demonstrate understanding of the meanings		
6. Word Roots Identify word roots as the base of words, which can give clues about a word's meaning		
7. Homographs Choose the correct meaning of a homograph used in a sentence		
8. Parts of Speech Identify words as nouns, verbs, adjectives, or adverbs by their use in a sentence		
9. Similes Choose the correct word or phrase to complete a simile		
10. Analogies Identify the relationship between objects in an analogy		
11. Main Idea and Details Identify the main idea and details in a paragraph		
12. Fact or Opinion? Distinguish between fact and opinion in text		

Take It to Your Seat Centers

Alphabetical Order

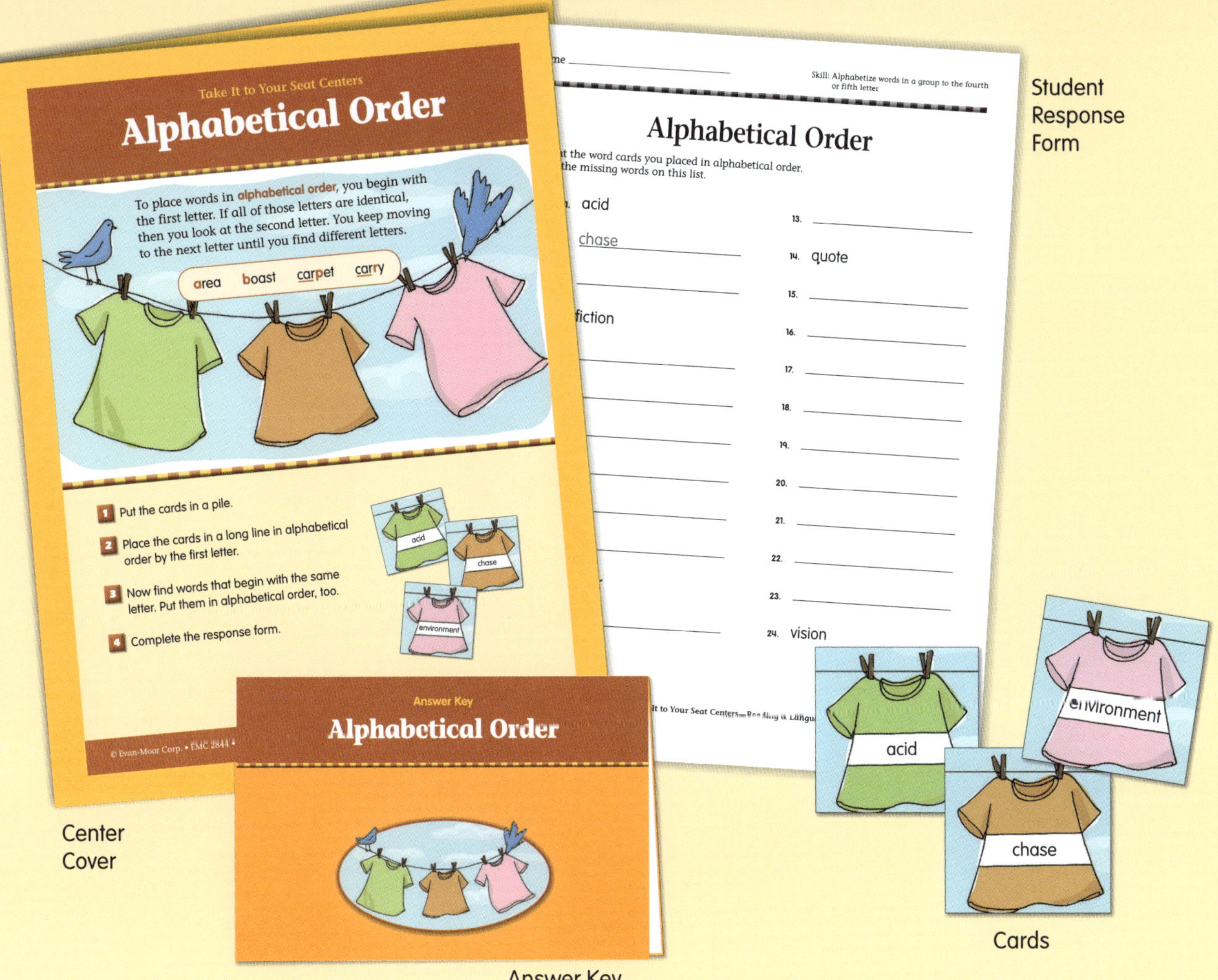

Student Response Form

Center Cover

Answer Key

Cards

Skill
Alphabetize words in a group to the fourth or fifth letter

Prepare the Center
Follow the directions on page 3.

Introduce the Center
Demonstrate how to use the center. State the goal: *You will place the word cards in alphabetical order by looking at just the first letter. Then you will take word cards that have the same first letter and use the second letter to order them. If the second letter is the same, use the third letter, and so on, until all the cards are in order.*

Name ______________________

Skill: Alphabetize words in a group to the fourth or fifth letter

Alphabetical Order

Look at the word cards you placed in alphabetical order.
Fill in the missing words on this list.

1. acid
2. chase
3. ______
4. fiction
5. ______
6. ______
7. ______
8. ______
9. ______
10. ______
11. owner
12. ______
13. ______
14. quote
15. ______
16. ______
17. ______
18. ______
19. ______
20. ______
21. ______
22. ______
23. ______
24. vision

Take It to Your Seat Centers

Alphabetical Order

To place words in **alphabetical order**, you begin with the first letter. If all of those letters are identical, then you look at the second letter. You keep moving to the next letter until you find different letters.

area boast carpet carry

1. Put the cards in a pile.
2. Place the cards in a long line in alphabetical order by the first letter.
3. Now find words that begin with the same letter. Put them in alphabetical order, too.
4. Complete the response form.

Response Form

Alphabetical Order

Look at the word cards you placed in alphabetical order.
Fill in the missing words on this list.

1. acid
2. chase
3. environment
4. fiction
5. grouch
6. ground
7. hyena
8. hypnotic
9. morning
10. mortar
11. owner
12. package
13. plaster
14. quote
15. radar
16. radial
17. radiate
18. radio
19. sanitary
20. sausage
21. save
22. science
23. scissors
24. vision

(fold)

Answer Key

Alphabetical Order

Answer Key

Alphabetical Order

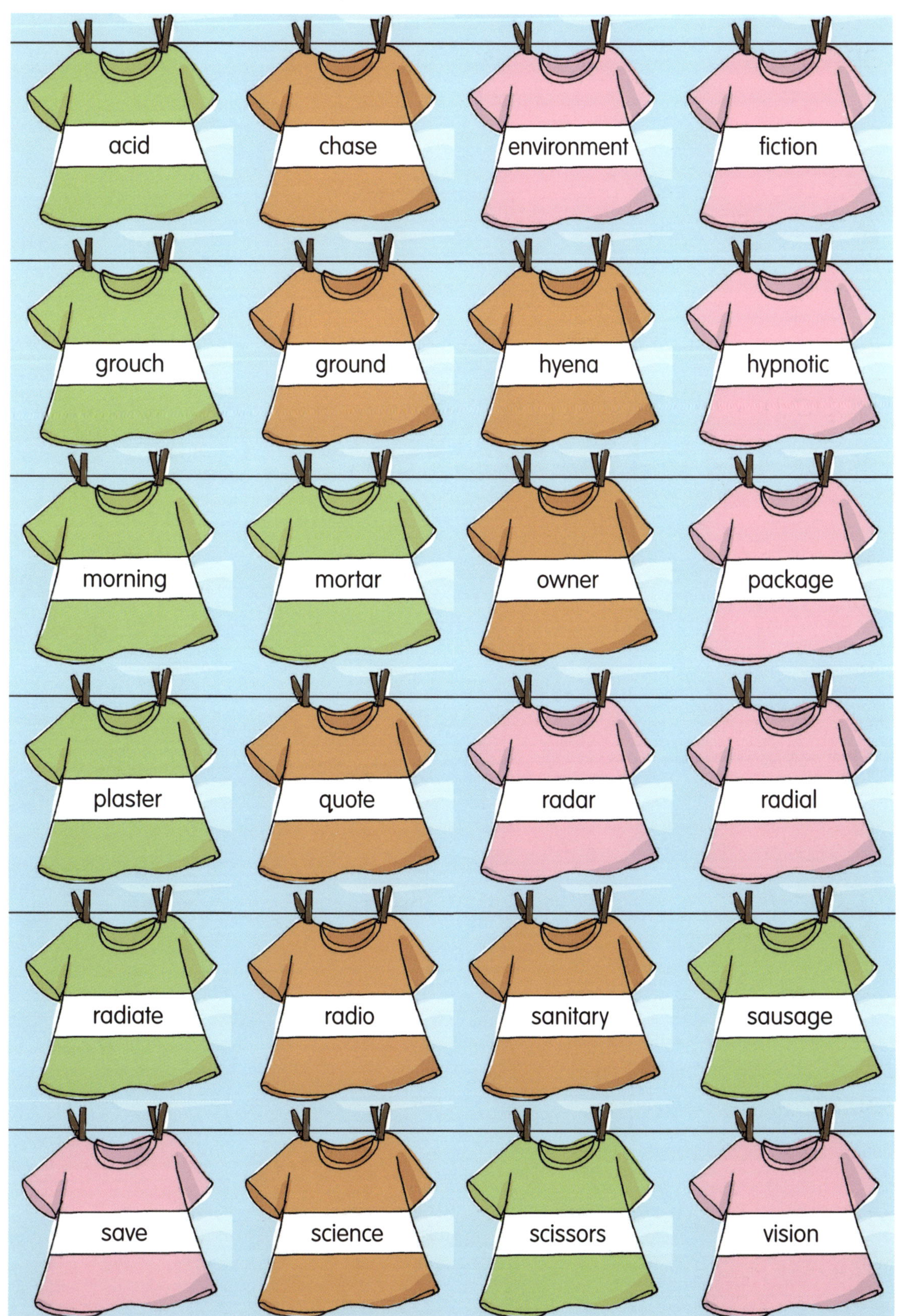

acid
chase
environment
fiction
grouch
ground
hyena
hypnotic
mortar
morning
owner
package

Alphabetical Order

Take It to Your Seat Centers
Reading & Language
EMC 2844 • © Evan-Moor Corp.

Alphabetical Order

Take It to Your Seat Centers
Reading & Language
EMC 2844 • © Evan-Moor Corp.

Alphabetical Order

Take It to Your Seat Centers
Reading & Language
EMC 2844 • © Evan-Moor Corp.

Alphabetical Order

Take It to Your Seat Centers
Reading & Language
EMC 2844 • © Evan-Moor Corp.

Alphabetical Order

Take It to Your Seat Centers
Reading & Language
EMC 2844 • © Evan-Moor Corp.

Alphabetical Order

Take It to Your Seat Centers
Reading & Language
EMC 2844 • © Evan-Moor Corp.

Alphabetical Order

Take It to Your Seat Centers
Reading & Language
EMC 2844 • © Evan-Moor Corp.

Alphabetical Order

Take It to Your Seat Centers
Reading & Language
EMC 2844 • © Evan-Moor Corp.

Alphabetical Order

Take It to Your Seat Centers
Reading & Language
EMC 2844 • © Evan-Moor Corp.

Alphabetical Order

Take It to Your Seat Centers
Reading & Language
EMC 2844 • © Evan-Moor Corp.

Alphabetical Order

Take It to Your Seat Centers
Reading & Language
EMC 2844 • © Evan-Moor Corp.

Alphabetical Order

Take It to Your Seat Centers
Reading & Language
EMC 2844 • © Evan-Moor Corp.

plaster
quote
radar
radial
radiate
radio
sanitary
save
sausage
scissors
science
vision

Alphabetical Order

Take It to Your Seat Centers
Reading & Language

Alphabetical Order

Take It to Your Seat Centers
Reading & Language
EMC 2844 • © Evan-Moor Corp.

Alphabetical Order

Take It to Your Seat Centers
Reading & Language
EMC 2844 • © Evan-Moor Corp.

Alphabetical Order

Take It to Your Seat Centers
Reading & Language
EMC 2844 • © Evan-Moor Corp.

Alphabetical Order

Take It to Your Seat Centers
Reading & Language
EMC 2844 • © Evan-Moor Corp.

Alphabetical Order

Take It to Your Seat Centers
Reading & Language
EMC 2844 • © Evan-Moor Corp.

Alphabetical Order

Take It to Your Seat Centers
Reading & Language
EMC 2844 • © Evan-Moor Corp.

Alphabetical Order

Take It to Your Seat Centers
Reading & Language
EMC 2844 • © Evan-Moor Corp.

Alphabetical Order

Take It to Your Seat Centers
Reading & Language
EMC 2844 • © Evan-Moor Corp.

Alphabetical Order

Take It to Your Seat Centers
Reading & Language
EMC 2844 • © Evan-Moor Corp.

Alphabetical Order

Take It to Your Seat Centers
Reading & Language
EMC 2844 • © Evan-Moor Corp.

Alphabetical Order

Take It to Your Seat Centers
Reading & Language
EMC 2844 • © Evan-Moor Corp.

Take It to Your Seat Centers

Synonyms/ Antonyms

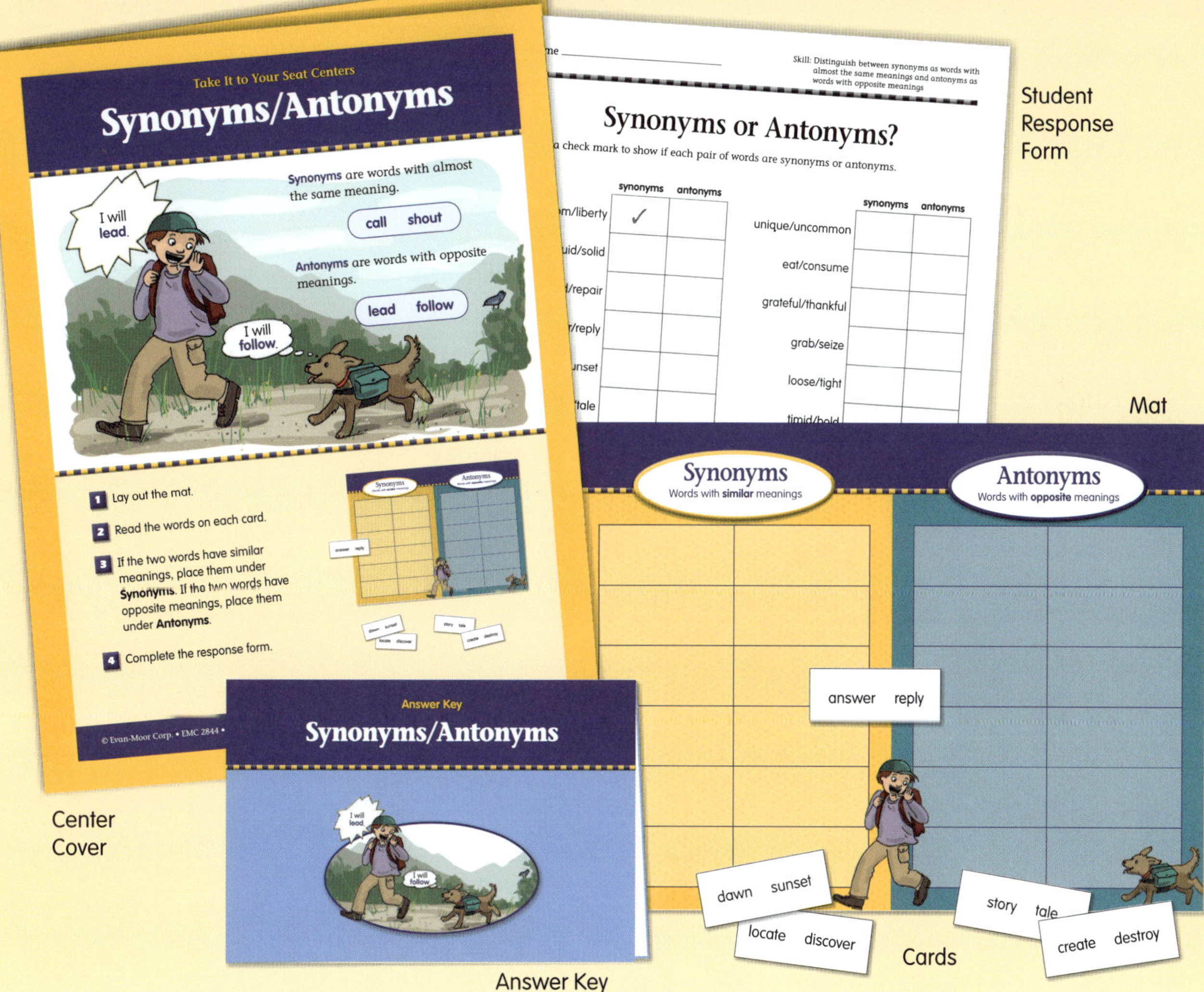

Skill
Distinguish between synonyms as words with almost the same meanings and antonyms as words with opposite meanings

Prepare the Center
Follow the directions on page 3.

Introduce the Center
Demonstrate how to use the center. State the goal: *You will read each word pair and decide if the words are synonyms or antonyms, then place the card on the correct side of the mat.*

Name ______________________

Skill: Distinguish between synonyms as words with almost the same meanings and antonyms as words with opposite meanings

Synonyms or Antonyms?

Make a check mark to show if each pair of words are synonyms or antonyms.

	synonyms	antonyms
freedom/liberty	✓	
liquid/solid		
mend/repair		
answer/reply		
dawn/sunset		
story/tale		
divide/separate		
greedy/generous		
vanish/appear		
answer/question		
innocent/guilty		
locate/discover		

	synonyms	antonyms
unique/uncommon		
eat/consume		
grateful/thankful		
grab/seize		
loose/tight		
timid/bold		
mistake/error		
problem/solution		
create/destroy		
follow/lead		
use/operate		
build/construct		

Take It to Your Seat Centers

Synonyms/Antonyms

I will **lead**.

I will **follow**.

Synonyms are words with almost the same meaning.

call shout

Antonyms are words with opposite meanings.

lead follow

1. Lay out the mat.
2. Read the words on each card.
3. If the two words have similar meanings, place them under **Synonyms**. If the two words have opposite meanings, place them under **Antonyms**.
4. Complete the response form.

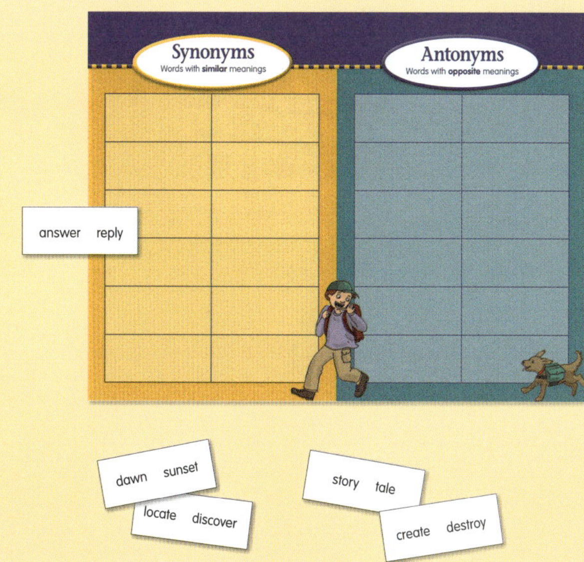

Synonyms or Antonyms?

Make a check mark to show if each pair of words are synonyms or antonyms.

	synonyms	antonyms
freedom/liberty	✓	
liquid/solid		✓
mend/repair	✓	
answer/reply	✓	
dawn/sunset		✓
story/tale	✓	
divide/separate	✓	
greedy/generous		✓
vanish/appear		✓
answer/question		✓
innocent/guilty		✓
locate/discover	✓	

	synonyms	antonyms
unique/uncommon	✓	
eat/consume	✓	
grateful/thankful	✓	
grab/seize	✓	
loose/tight		✓
timid/bold		✓
mistake/error	✓	
problem/solution		✓
create/destroy		✓
follow/lead		✓
use/operate	✓	
build/construct	✓	

Response Form

(fold)

Answer Key

Synonyms/Antonyms

Answer Key

Synonyms/Antonyms

Synonyms

Words with **similar** meanings

answer reply	story tale
locate discover	grab seize
divide separate	build construct
eat consume	mistake error
grateful thankful	mend repair
freedom liberty	use operate

Antonyms

Words with **opposite** meanings

dawn sunset	create destroy
answer question	problem solution
follow lead	vanish appear
greedy generous	loose tight
innocent guilty	timid bold
liquid solid	unique uncommon

Synonyms

Words with **similar** meanings

Antonyms

Words with **opposite** meanings

Synonyms/Antonyms

Take It to Your Seat Centers
Reading & Language

Synonyms/Antonyms

Take It to Your Seat Centers
Reading & Language
EMC 2844 • © Evan-Moor Corp.

Synonyms/Antonyms

Take It to Your Seat Centers
Reading & Language
EMC 2844 • © Evan-Moor Corp.

Synonyms/Antonyms

Take It to Your Seat Centers
Reading & Language
EMC 2844 • © Evan-Moor Corp.

Synonyms/Antonyms

Take It to Your Seat Centers
Reading & Language
EMC 2844 • © Evan-Moor Corp.

Synonyms/Antonyms

Take It to Your Seat Centers
Reading & Language
EMC 2844 • © Evan-Moor Corp.

Synonyms/Antonyms

Take It to Your Seat Centers
Reading & Language
EMC 2844 • © Evan-Moor Corp.

Synonyms/Antonyms

Take It to Your Seat Centers
Reading & Language
EMC 2844 • © Evan-Moor Corp.

Synonyms/Antonyms

Take It to Your Seat Centers
Reading & Language
EMC 2844 • © Evan-Moor Corp.

Synonyms/Antonyms

Take It to Your Seat Centers
Reading & Language
EMC 2844 • © Evan-Moor Corp.

Synonyms/Antonyms

Take It to Your Seat Centers
Reading & Language
EMC 2844 • © Evan-Moor Corp.

Synonyms/Antonyms

Take It to Your Seat Centers
Reading & Language
EMC 2844 • © Evan-Moor Corp.

dawn sunset	create destroy
answer question	problem solution
follow lead	vanish appear
greedy generous	loose tight
innocent guilty	timid bold
liquid solid	unique uncommon

Synonyms/Antonyms

Take It to Your Seat Centers
Reading & Language
EMC 2844 • © Evan-Moor Corp.

Synonyms/Antonyms

Take It to Your Seat Centers
Reading & Language
EMC 2844 • © Evan-Moor Corp.

Synonyms/Antonyms

Take It to Your Seat Centers
Reading & Language
EMC 2844 • © Evan-Moor Corp.

Synonyms/Antonyms

Take It to Your Seat Centers
Reading & Language
EMC 2844 • © Evan-Moor Corp.

Synonyms/Antonyms

Take It to Your Seat Centers
Reading & Language
EMC 2844 • © Evan-Moor Corp.

Synonyms/Antonyms

Take It to Your Seat Centers
Reading & Language
EMC 2844 • © Evan-Moor Corp.

Synonyms/Antonyms

Take It to Your Seat Centers
Reading & Language
EMC 2844 • © Evan-Moor Corp.

Synonyms/Antonyms

Take It to Your Seat Centers
Reading & Language
EMC 2844 • © Evan-Moor Corp.

Synonyms/Antonyms

Take It to Your Seat Centers
Reading & Language
EMC 2844 • © Evan-Moor Corp.

Synonyms/Antonyms

Take It to Your Seat Centers
Reading & Language
EMC 2844 • © Evan-Moor Corp.

Synonyms/Antonyms

Take It to Your Seat Centers
Reading & Language
EMC 2844 • © Evan-Moor Corp.

Synonyms/Antonyms

Take It to Your Seat Centers
Reading & Language
EMC 2844 • © Evan-Moor Corp.

Take It to Your Seat Centers

Sequencing

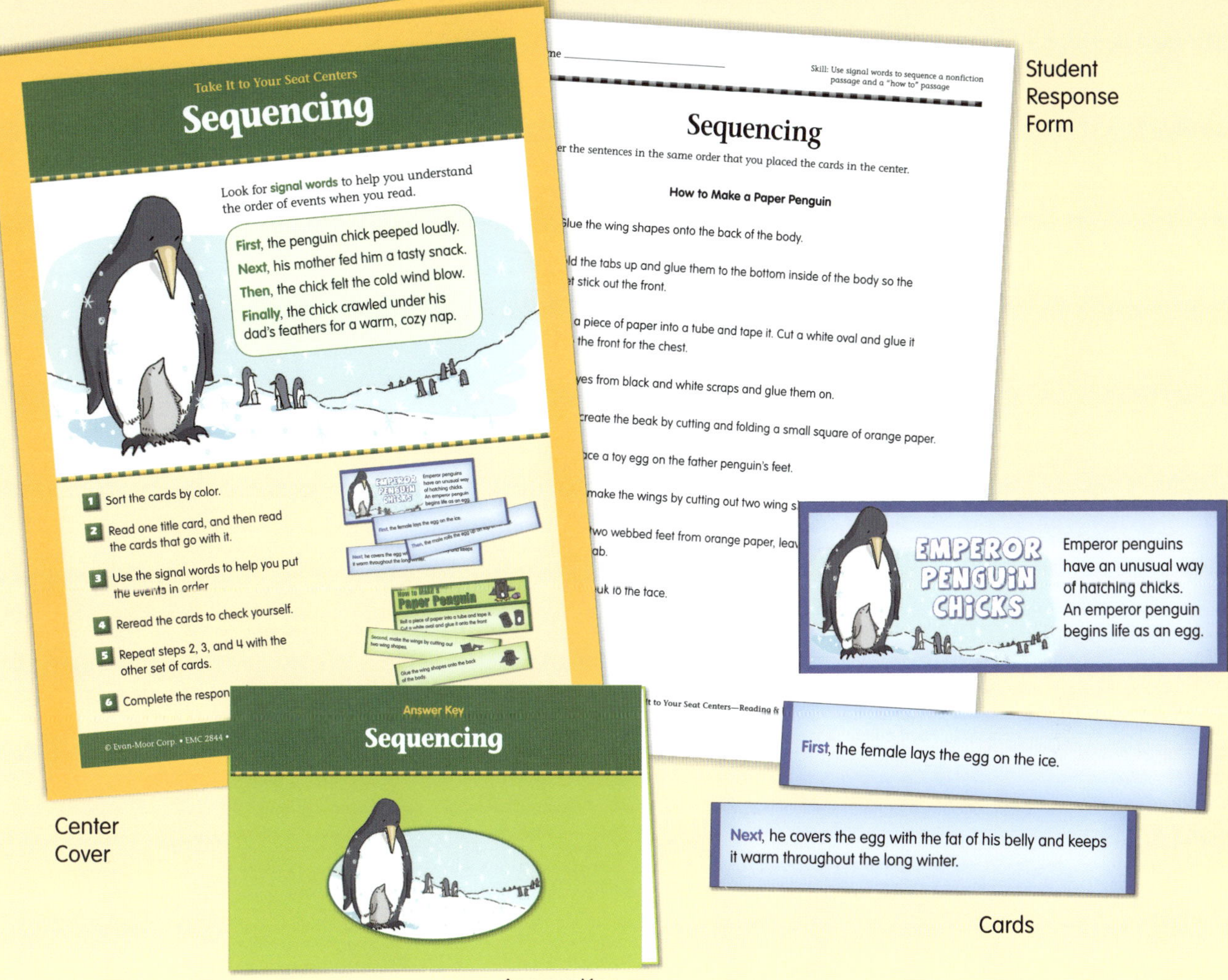

Skill
Use signal words to sequence a nonfiction passage and a "how to" passage

Prepare the Center
Follow the directions on page 3.

Introduce the Center
Demonstrate how to use the center. State the goal: *You will read two title cards and sentences that go with them. Then you will look for signal words in the sentences and place them in order to show a process.*

Name ______________________________

Skill: Use signal words to sequence a nonfiction passage and a "how to" passage

Sequencing

Number the sentences in the same order that you placed the cards in the center.

How to Make a Paper Penguin

_____ Glue the wing shapes onto the back of the body.

_____ Fold the tabs up and glue them to the bottom inside of the body so the feet stick out the front.

_____ Roll a piece of paper into a tube and tape it. Cut a white oval and glue it onto the front for the chest.

_____ Cut eyes from black and white scraps and glue them on.

_____ Then, create the beak by cutting and folding a small square of orange paper.

_____ Last, place a toy egg on the father penguin's feet.

_____ Second, make the wings by cutting out two wing shapes.

_____ Next, cut two webbed feet from orange paper, leaving a bit extra on each one for a tab.

_____ Glue the beak to the face.

Sequencing

Look for **signal words** to help you understand the order of events when you read.

First, the penguin chick peeped loudly.

Next, his mother fed him a tasty snack.

Then, the chick felt the cold wind blow.

Finally, the chick crawled under his dad's feathers for a warm, cozy nap.

1. Sort the cards by color.
2. Read one title card, and then read the cards that go with it.
3. Use the signal words to help you put the events in order.
4. Reread the cards to check yourself.
5. Repeat steps 2, 3, and 4 with the other set of cards.
6. Complete the response form.

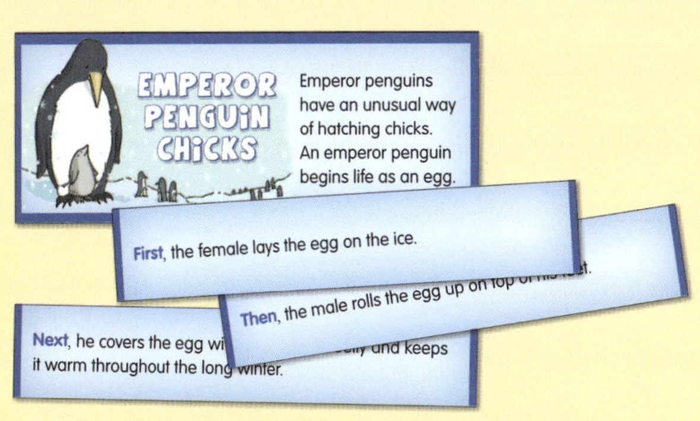

Sequencing

Answer Key

(fold)

Response Form

Sequencing

Number the sentences in the same order that you placed the cards in the center.

How to Make a Paper Penguin

3 Glue the wing shapes onto the back of the body.

5 Fold the tabs up and glue them to the bottom inside of the body so the feet stick out the front.

1 Roll a piece of paper into a tube and tape it. Cut a white oval and glue it onto the front for the chest.

8 Cut eyes from black and white scraps and glue them on.

6 Then, create the beak by cutting and folding a small square of orange paper.

9 Last, place a toy egg on the father penguin's feet.

2 Second, make the wings by cutting out two wing shapes.

4 Next, cut two webbed feet from orange paper, leaving a bit extra on each one for a tab.

7 Glue the beak to the face.

Answer Key

Sequencing

Emperor Penguin Chicks

Emperor penguins have an unusual way of hatching chicks. An emperor penguin begins life as an egg.

First, the female lays the egg on the ice.

Then, the male rolls the egg up on top of his feet.

Next, he covers the egg with the fat of his belly and keeps it warm throughout the long winter.

At hatching time, it can take two or three days for a chick to break the thick eggshell.

When the chick finally does hatch, it must be protected.

One parent hunts for food while the other parent watches the chick.

Finally, when the young penguin is big enough, it joins its parents in the sea. There the young penguin learns to swim and hunt for its food.

How to Make a Paper Penguin

Roll a piece of paper into a tube and tape it. Cut a white oval and glue it onto the front for the chest.

Second, make the wings by cutting out two wing shapes.

Glue the wing shapes onto the back of the body.

Next, cut two webbed feet from orange paper, leaving a bit extra on each one for a tab.

Fold the tabs up and glue them to the bottom inside of the body so the feet stick out the front.

Then, create the beak by cutting and folding a small square of orange paper.

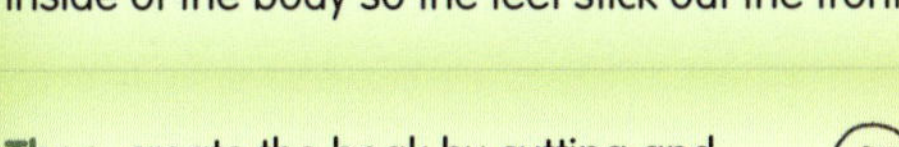

Glue the beak to the face.

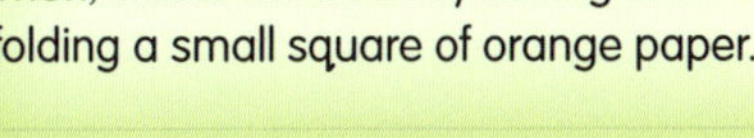
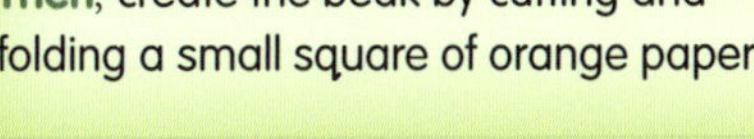
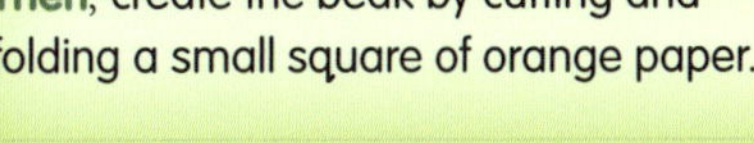
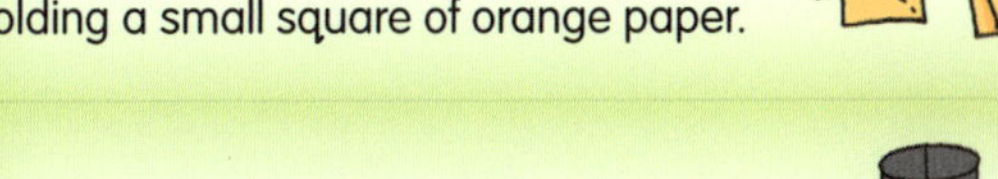

Cut eyes from black and white scraps and glue them on.

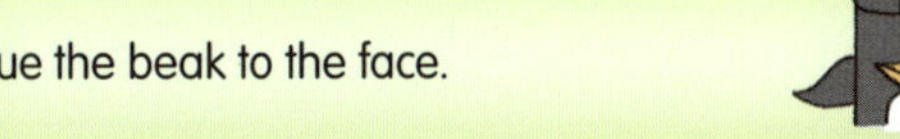
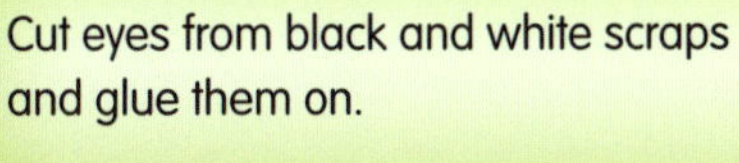

Last, place a toy egg on the father penguin's feet.

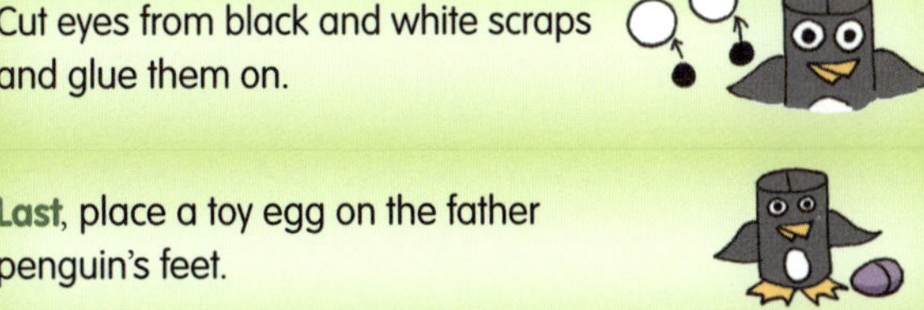
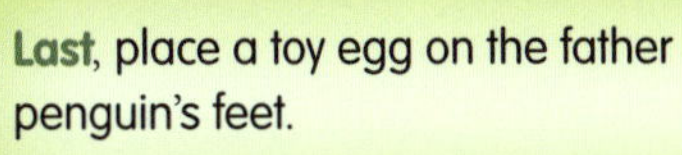

Emperor penguins have an unusual way of hatching chicks. An emperor penguin begins life as an egg.

First, the female lays the egg on the ice.

Then, the male rolls the egg up on top of his feet.

Next, he covers the egg with the fat of his belly and keeps it warm throughout the long winter.

At hatching time, it can take two or three days for a chick to break the thick eggshell.

When the chick finally does hatch, it must be protected.

Sequencing

Take It to Your Seat
Reading & Language Centers

Sequencing

Take It to Your Seat
Reading & Language Centers
EMC 2844 • © Evan-Moor Corp.

Sequencing

Take It to Your Seat
Reading & Language Centers
EMC 2844 • © Evan-Moor Corp.

Sequencing

Take It to Your Seat
Reading & Language Centers
EMC 2844 • © Evan-Moor Corp.

Sequencing

Take It to Your Seat
Reading & Language Centers
EMC 2844 • © Evan-Moor Corp.

Sequencing

Take It to Your Seat
Reading & Language Centers
EMC 2844 • © Evan-Moor Corp.

One parent hunts for food while the other parent watches the chick.

Finally, when the young penguin is big enough, it joins its parents in the sea. There the young penguin learns to swim and hunt for its food.

How to Make a Paper Penguin

Roll a piece of paper into a tube and tape it. Cut a white oval and glue it onto the front for the chest.

Second, make the wings by cutting out two wing shapes.

Glue the wing shapes onto the back of the body.

Sequencing

Take It to Your Seat
Reading & Language Centers
EMC 2844 • © Evan-Moor Corp.

Sequencing

Take It to Your Seat
Reading & Language Centers
EMC 2844 • © Evan-Moor Corp.

Sequencing

Take It to Your Seat
Reading & Language Centers
EMC 2844 • © Evan-Moor Corp.

Sequencing

Take It to Your Seat
Reading & Language Centers
EMC 2844 • © Evan-Moor Corp.

Sequencing

Take It to Your Seat
Reading & Language Centers
EMC 2844 • © Evan-Moor Corp.

Sequencing

Take It to Your Seat
Reading & Language Centers
EMC 2844 • © Evan-Moor Corp.

Next, cut two webbed feet from orange paper, leaving a bit extra on each one for a tab.

Fold the tabs up and glue them to the bottom inside of the body so the feet stick out the front.

Then, create the beak by cutting and folding a small square of orange paper.

Glue the beak to the face.

Cut eyes from black and white scraps and glue them on.

Last, place a toy egg on the father penguin's feet.

Sequencing

Take It to Your Seat
Reading & Language Centers
EMC 2844 • © Evan-Moor Corp.

Sequencing

Take It to Your Seat
Reading & Language Centers
EMC 2844 • © Evan-Moor Corp.

Sequencing

Take It to Your Seat
Reading & Language Centers
EMC 2844 • © Evan-Moor Corp.

Sequencing

Take It to Your Seat
Reading & Language Centers
EMC 2844 • © Evan-Moor Corp.

Sequencing

Take It to Your Seat
Reading & Language Centers
EMC 2844 • © Evan-Moor Corp.

Sequencing

Take It to Your Seat
Reading & Language Centers
EMC 2844 • © Evan-Moor Corp.

Take It to Your Seat Centers

Prefixes

Skill

Form new words from a prefix and a base word, and demonstrate understanding of the meanings

Prepare the Center

Follow the directions on page 3.

Introduce the Center

Demonstrate how to use the center. State the goal: *You will make new words by placing the base word cards under the correct prefixes (**fore-**, **co-**, **super-**, **im-**, **sub-**, **multi-**) on the mats.*

Name ______________________________

Skill: Form new words from a prefix and a base word, and demonstrate understanding of the meanings

Prefixes

Circle the prefix in each word.

1. imperfect
2. submarine
3. coexist
4. immobile
5. multipurpose
6. supersonic
7. cooperation
8. forewarned
9. supernatural
10. subway
11. immature
12. submerge
13. foresee
14. supermarket
15. multimedia
16. forehead
17. copilot
18. multicultural

Use words from above to complete each sentence.

1. The siren ____________________ us of the speeding fire truck before we saw it.
2. The deer became ____________________ when the headlights hit it.
3. Our dog and cat learned how to ____________________.
4. Rockets travel at ____________________ speeds.
5. ____________________ the pot in soapy water to soak off the burned-on food.
6. We had our basketball game in the school's ____________________ room.
7. I told my brother he was ____________________ to cry about his lost whistle.

Prefixes

Now you see me!

appear

Now you don't!

disappear

A **prefix** is a word part added at the beginning of a word. A prefix changes the meaning of the word.

1. Lay out the mats.
2. Put the cards in a pile. Read one card at a time.
3. Find the prefix on a mat that correctly fits with each word. Place the card next to that prefix.
4. Read the new word. Think about its meaning.
5. Complete the response form.

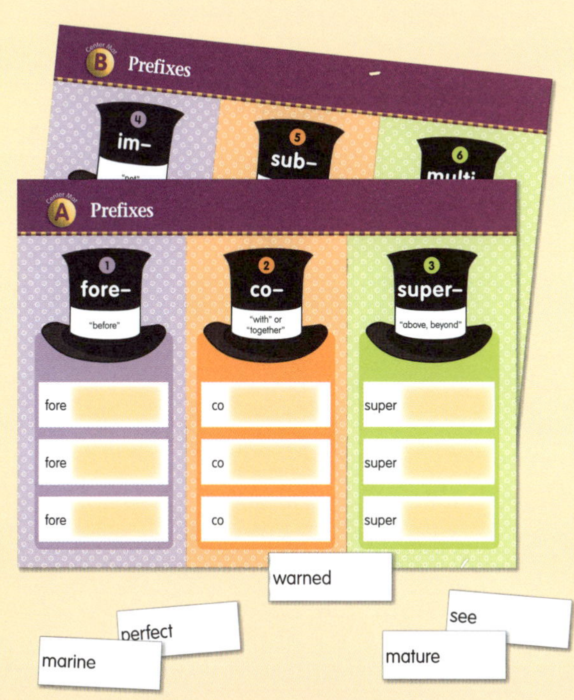

Prefixes

Answer Key

(fold)

Response Form

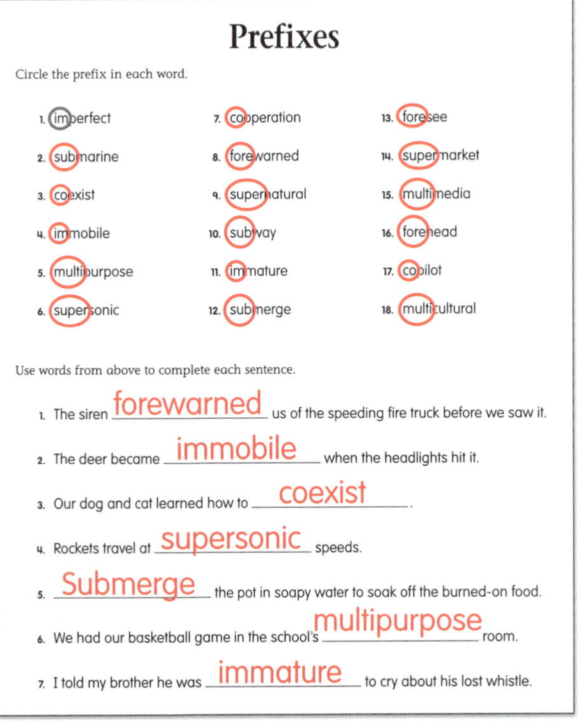

Prefixes

Circle the prefix in each word.

1. imperfect	7. cooperation	13. foresee
2. submarine	8. forewarned	14. supermarket
3. coexist	9. supernatural	15. multimedia
4. immobile	10. subway	16. forehead
5. multipurpose	11. immature	17. copilot
6. supersonic	12. submerge	18. multicultural

Use words from above to complete each sentence.

1. The siren forewarned us of the speeding fire truck before we saw it.
2. The deer became immobile when the headlights hit it.
3. Our dog and cat learned how to coexist.
4. Rockets travel at supersonic speeds.
5. Submerge the pot in soapy water to soak off the burned-on food.
6. We had our basketball game in the school's multipurpose room.
7. I told my brother he was immature to cry about his lost whistle.

Answer Key

Prefixes

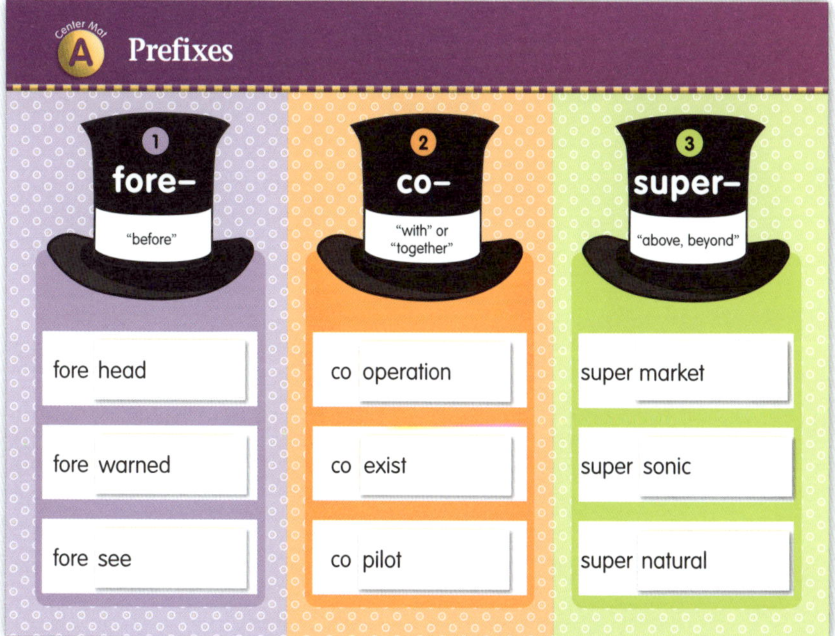

Center Mat B Prefixes

4 im– "not"	5 sub– "under, below, smaller"	6 multi– "many"
im mobile	sub marine	multi cultural
im perfect	sub way	multi media
im mature	sub merge	multi purpose

Center Mat A

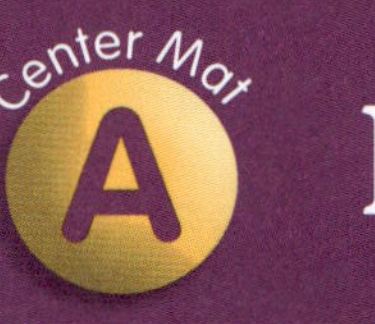

Prefixes

1 fore– "before"	2 co– "with" or "together"	3 super– "above, beyond"
fore	co	super
fore	co	super
fore	co	super

Prefixes

4 im- "not"	5 sub- "under, below, smaller"	6 multi- "many"
im	sub	multi
im	sub	multi
im	sub	multi

perfect	mature	mobile
marine	way	merge
purpose	media	cultural
see	warned	head
operation	exist	pilot
sonic	market	natural

Prefixes

Take It to Your Seat Centers
Reading & Language
EMC 2844 • © Evan-Moor Corp.

Prefixes

Take It to Your Seat Centers
Reading & Language
EMC 2844 • © Evan-Moor Corp.

Prefixes

Take It to Your Seat Centers
Reading & Language
EMC 2844 • © Evan-Moor Corp.

Prefixes

Take It to Your Seat Centers
Reading & Language
EMC 2844 • © Evan-Moor Corp.

Prefixes

Take It to Your Seat Centers
Reading & Language
EMC 2844 • © Evan-Moor Corp.

Prefixes

Take It to Your Seat Centers
Reading & Language
EMC 2844 • © Evan-Moor Corp.

Prefixes

Take It to Your Seat Centers
Reading & Language
EMC 2844 • © Evan-Moor Corp.

Prefixes

Take It to Your Seat Centers
Reading & Language
EMC 2844 • © Evan-Moor Corp.

Prefixes

Take It to Your Seat Centers
Reading & Language
EMC 2844 • © Evan-Moor Corp.

Prefixes

Take It to Your Seat Centers
Reading & Language
EMC 2844 • © Evan-Moor Corp.

Prefixes

Take It to Your Seat Centers
Reading & Language
EMC 2844 • © Evan-Moor Corp.

Prefixes

Take It to Your Seat Centers
Reading & Language
EMC 2844 • © Evan-Moor Corp.

Prefixes

Take It to Your Seat Centers
Reading & Language
EMC 2844 • © Evan-Moor Corp.

Prefixes

Take It to Your Seat Centers
Reading & Language
EMC 2844 • © Evan-Moor Corp.

Prefixes

Take It to Your Seat Centers
Reading & Language
EMC 2844 • © Evan-Moor Corp.

Prefixes

Take It to Your Seat Centers
Reading & Language
EMC 2844 • © Evan-Moor Corp.

Prefixes

Take It to Your Seat Centers
Reading & Language
EMC 2844 • © Evan-Moor Corp.

Prefixes

Take It to Your Seat Centers
Reading & Language
EMC 2844 • © Evan-Moor Corp.

Take It to Your Seat Centers

Suffixes

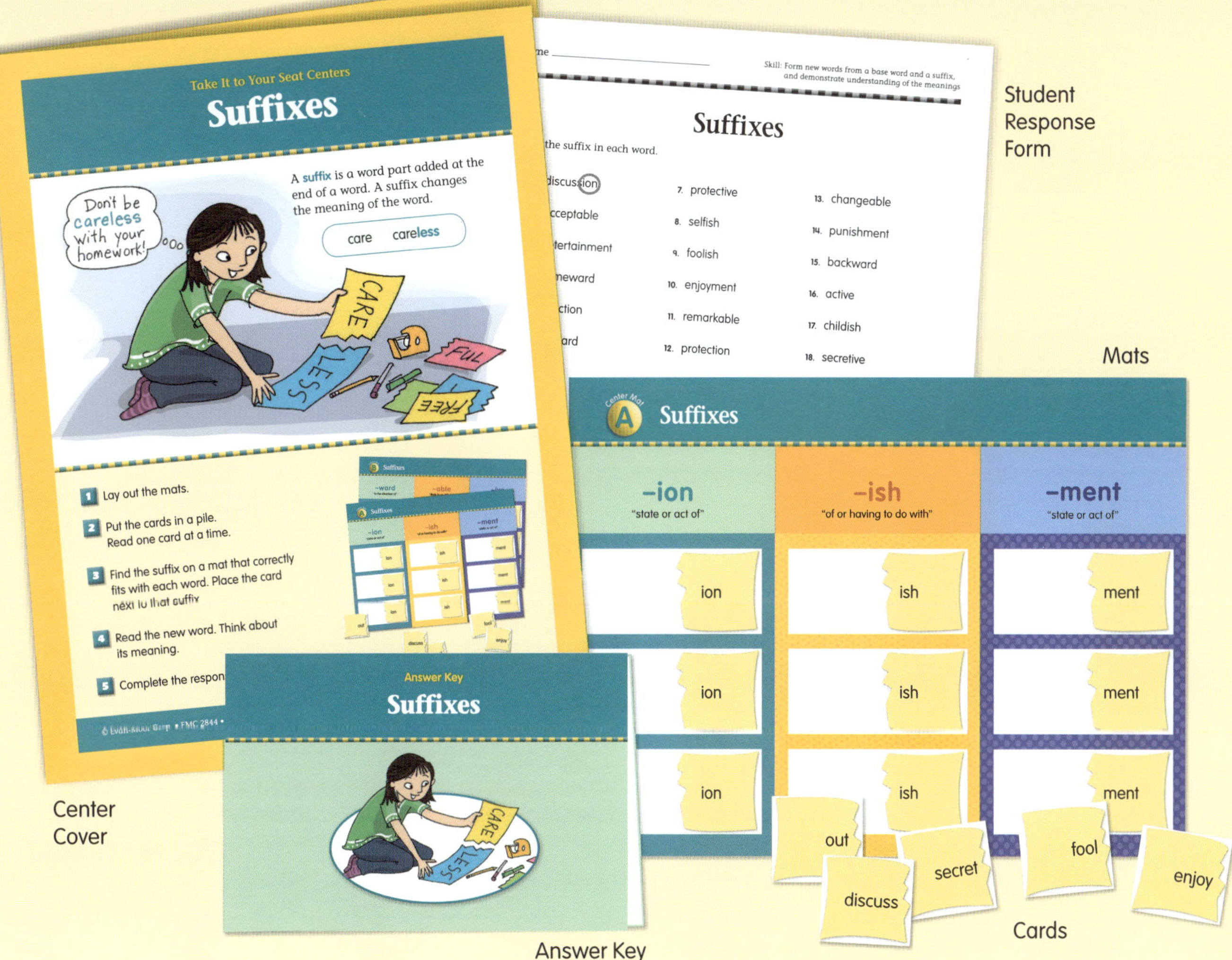

Skill
Form new words from a base word and a suffix, and demonstrate understanding of the meanings

Prepare the Center
Follow the directions on page 3.

Introduce the Center
Demonstrate how to use the center. State the goal: *You will make new words by placing the base word cards under the correct suffixes (**-ion**, **-ish**, **-ment**, **-ward**, **-able**, **-ive**) on the mats.*

Name ______________________

Skill: Form new words from a base word and a suffix, and demonstrate understanding of the meanings

Suffixes

Circle the suffix in each word.

1. discussion
2. acceptable
3. entertainment
4. homeward
5. selection
6. outward
7. protective
8. selfish
9. foolish
10. enjoyment
11. remarkable
12. protection
13. changeable
14. punishment
15. backward
16. active
17. childish
18. secretive

Use words from above to complete each sentence.

1. The judge will decide on a ______________________ to fit the crime.
2. Winning a gold medal in two sports is ______________________.
3. The horses began to run as soon as we turned ______________________.
4. The farmer's market has a large ______________________ of fresh produce.
5. My friend's dog is very ______________________ of the family.
6. It is not ______________________ to eat on the new couch.
7. My class had a ______________________ about how we could all help recycle.

Take It to Your Seat Centers

Suffixes

A **suffix** is a word part added at the end of a word. A suffix changes the meaning of the word.

care careless

1. Lay out the mats.
2. Put the cards in a pile. Read one card at a time.
3. Find the suffix on a mat that correctly fits with each word. Place the card next to that suffix.
4. Read the new word. Think about its meaning.
5. Complete the response form.

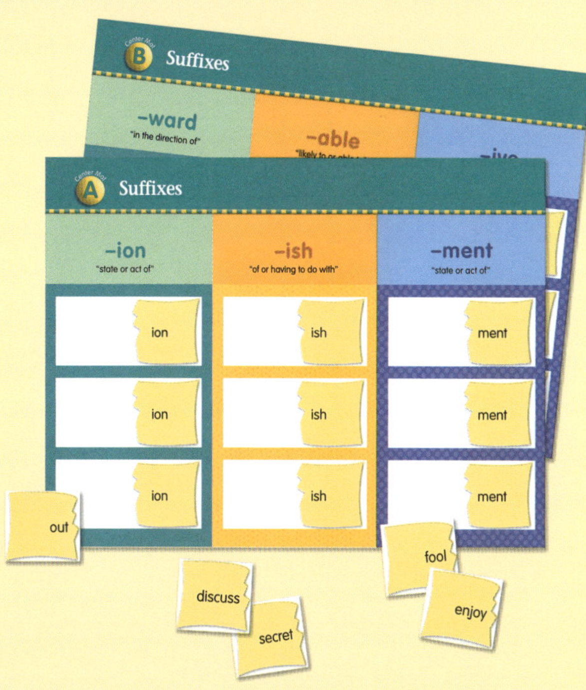

Answer Key

Suffixes

(fold)

Response Form

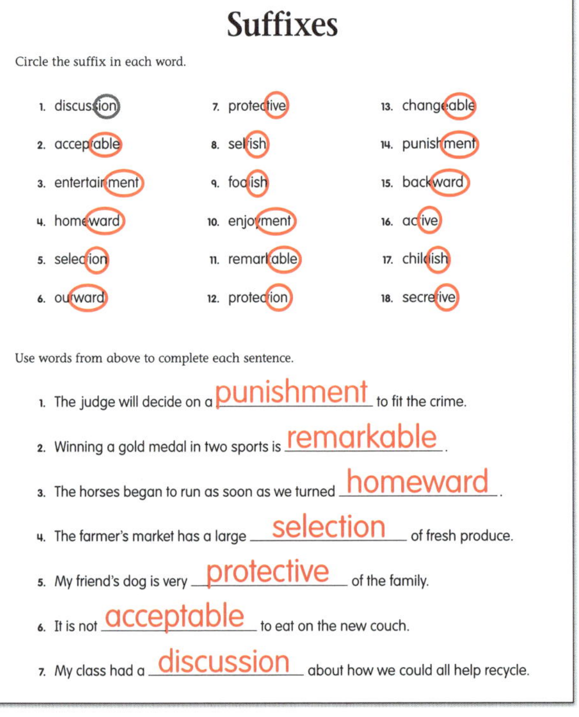

Suffixes

Circle the suffix in each word.

1. discussion
2. acceptable
3. entertainment
4. homeward
5. selection
6. outward
7. protective
8. selfish
9. foolish
10. enjoyment
11. remarkable
12. protection
13. changeable
14. punishment
15. backward
16. active
17. childish
18. secretive

Use words from above to complete each sentence.

1. The judge will decide on a punishment to fit the crime.
2. Winning a gold medal in two sports is remarkable.
3. The horses began to run as soon as we turned homeward.
4. The farmer's market has a large selection of fresh produce.
5. My friend's dog is very protective of the family.
6. It is not acceptable to eat on the new couch.
7. My class had a discussion about how we could all help recycle.

Answer Key

Suffixes

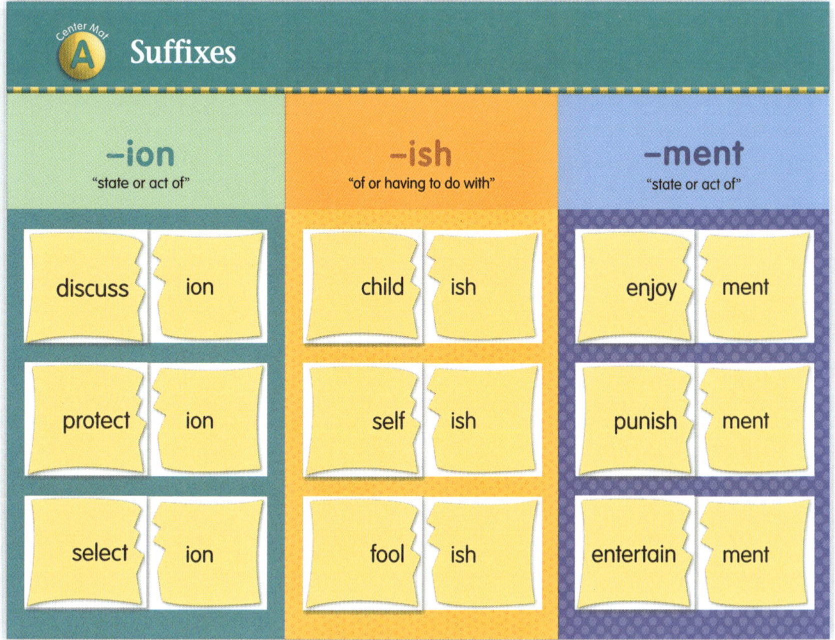

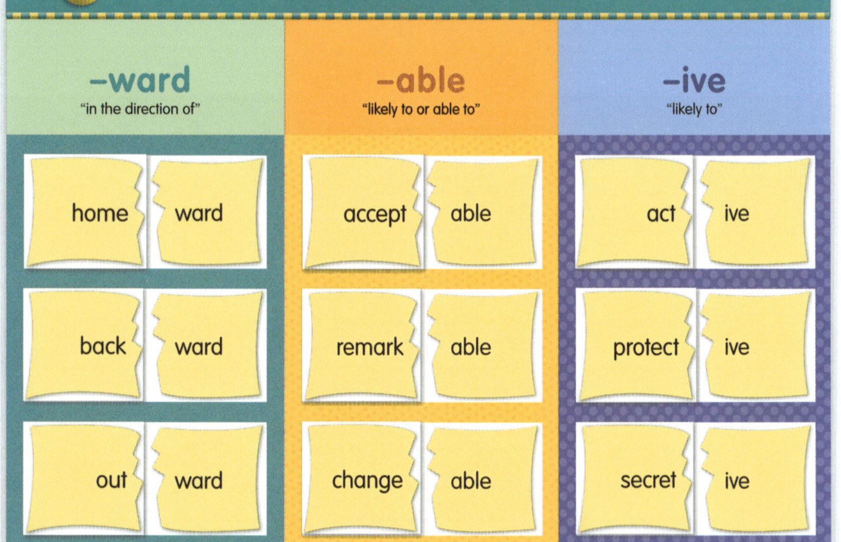

Suffixes

-ion "state or act of"	-ish "of or having to do with"	-ment "state or act of"
ion	ish	ment
ion	ish	ment
ion	ish	ment

Suffixes

–ward "in the direction of"	–able "likely to or able to"	–ive "likely to"
ward	able	ive
ward	able	ive
ward	able	ive

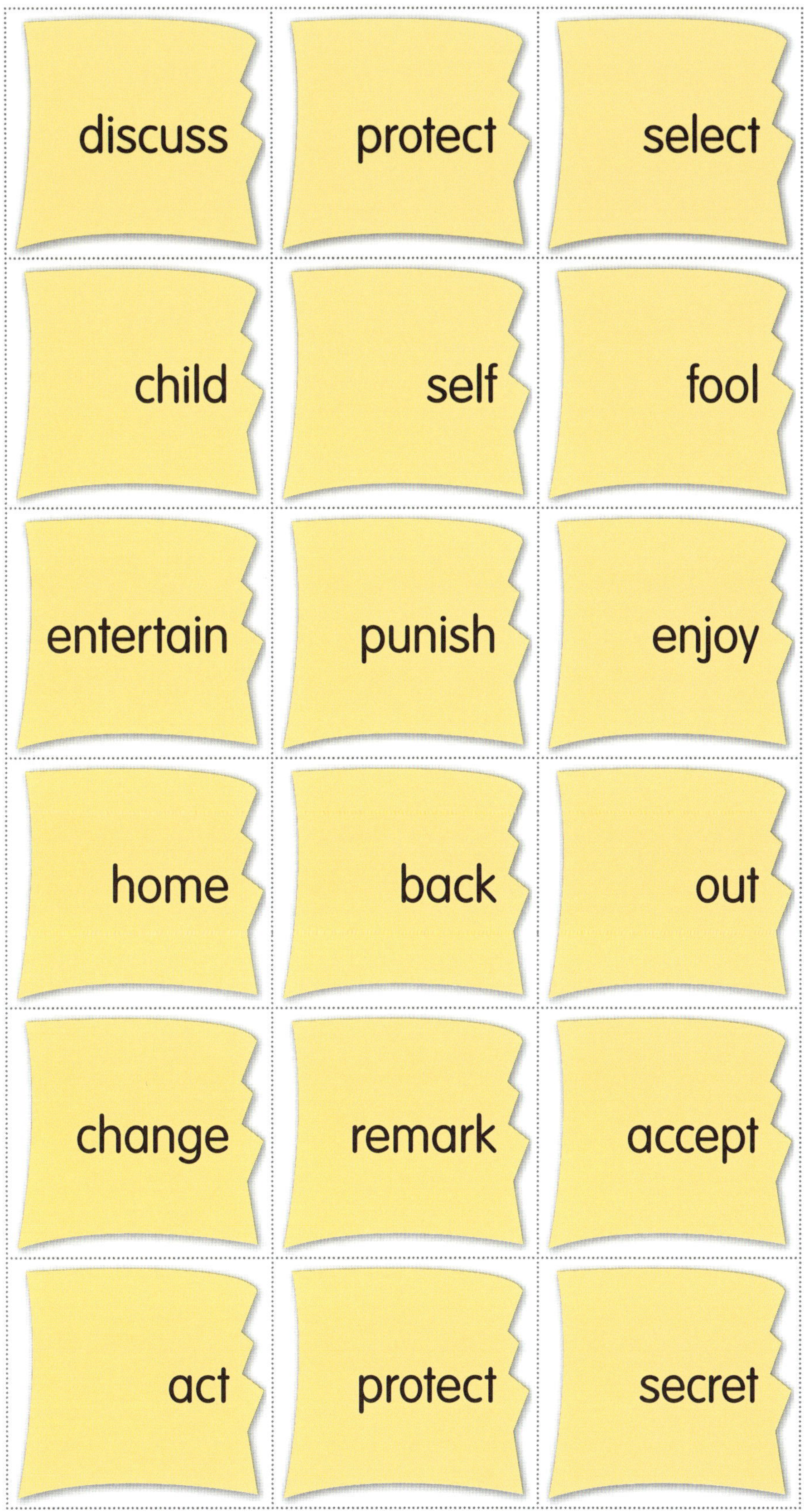
discuss
protect
select
child
self
fool
entertain
punish
enjoy
home
back
out
change
remark
accept
act
protect
secret

Suffixes

Take It to Your
Seat Centers
Reading & Language
EMC 2844
© Evan-Moor Corp.

Suffixes

Take It to Your
Seat Centers
Reading & Language
EMC 2844
© Evan-Moor Corp.

Suffixes

Take It to Your
Seat Centers
Reading & Language
EMC 2844
© Evan-Moor Corp.

Suffixes

Take It to Your
Seat Centers
Reading & Language
EMC 2844
© Evan-Moor Corp.

Suffixes

Take It to Your
Seat Centers
Reading & Language
EMC 2844
© Evan-Moor Corp.

Suffixes

Take It to Your
Seat Centers
Reading & Language
EMC 2844
© Evan-Moor Corp.

Suffixes

Take It to Your
Seat Centers
Reading & Language
EMC 2844
© Evan-Moor Corp.

Suffixes

Take It to Your
Seat Centers
Reading & Language
EMC 2844
© Evan-Moor Corp.

Suffixes

Take It to Your
Seat Centers
Reading & Language
EMC 2844
© Evan-Moor Corp.

Suffixes

Take It to Your
Seat Centers
Reading & Language
EMC 2844
© Evan-Moor Corp.

Suffixes

Take It to Your
Seat Centers
Reading & Language
EMC 2844
© Evan-Moor Corp.

Suffixes

Take It to Your
Seat Centers
Reading & Language
EMC 2844
© Evan-Moor Corp.

Suffixes

Take It to Your
Seat Centers
Reading & Language
EMC 2844
© Evan-Moor Corp.

Suffixes

Take It to Your
Seat Centers
Reading & Language
EMC 2844
© Evan-Moor Corp.

Suffixes

Take It to Your
Seat Centers
Reading & Language
EMC 2844
© Evan-Moor Corp.

Suffixes

Take It to Your
Seat Centers
Reading & Language
EMC 2844
© Evan-Moor Corp.

Suffixes

Take It to Your
Seat Centers
Reading & Language
EMC 2844
© Evan-Moor Corp.

Suffixes

Take It to Your
Seat Centers
Reading & Language
EMC 2844
© Evan-Moor Corp.

Take It to Your Seat Centers

Word Roots

Skill
Identify word roots as the base of words, which can give clues about a word's meaning

Prepare the Center
Follow the directions on page 3.

Introduce the Center
Demonstrate how to use the center. State the goal: *You will read each word card, look for its root, and then place the card next to the root on the mat that helps give the word its meaning.*

Name ______________________

Skill: Identify word roots as the base of words, which can give clues about a word's meaning

Word Roots

Circle the word root in each word.

1. speedometer
2. centimeter
3. manual
4. pedal
5. manufacture
6. describe
7. erect
8. pedestrian
9. bicycle
10. rectangle
11. terrain
12. aquatic
13. cyclone
14. contradict
15. thermostat
16. react
17. invisible
18. thermos
19. action
20. vision
21. dictate
22. territory
23. scribble
24. aquarium

Use words from above to complete each sentence.

1. My new glasses have given me improved ______________________.
2. My baby brother likes to ______________________ while I write.
3. I've seen a clown use his hands to ______________________ a bike!
4. The ______________________ measures how fast Mom is driving.
5. The state of Texas has miles of open ______________________.
6. The pool at the new ______________________ center is huge.

Take It to Your Seat Centers

Word Roots

Roots are word parts that form the base of words and can give clues to the words' meanings. Many English words originally came from Greek and Latin roots.

geo means "earth"
geography
Greek root

1. Lay out the mats.
2. Read one card at a time. Look for the word root.
3. Find the root on a mat that matches, and then place the card in a box next to that root.
4. Complete the response form.

Response Form

Word Roots

Circle the word root in each word.

1. speedometer
2. centimeter
3. manual
4. pedal
5. manufacture
6. describe
7. erect
8. pedestrian
9. bicycle
10. rectangle
11. terrain
12. aquatic
13. cyclone
14. contradict
15. thermostat
16. react
17. invisible
18. thermos
19. action
20. vision
21. dictate
22. territory
23. scribble
24. aquarium

Use words from above to complete each sentence.

1. My new glasses have given me improved vision.
2. My baby brother likes to scribble while I write.
3. I've seen a clown use his hands to pedal a bike!
4. The speedometer measures how fast Mom is driving.
5. The state of Texas has miles of open territory.
6. The pool at the new aquatic center is huge.

(fold)

Answer Key

Word Roots

Answer Key

Word Roots

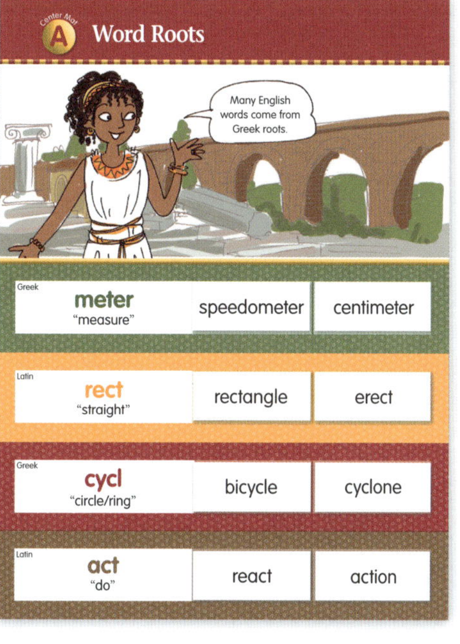

C

Center Mat A

Word Roots

Greek **meter** "measure"		
Latin **rect** "straight"		
Greek **cycl** "circle/ring"		
Latin **act** "do"		

Word Roots

Latin **vis** "see"		
Latin **dict** "speak"		
Greek **therm** "heat"		
Latin **man** "hand"		

Center Mat C

Word Roots

Latin **ped** "foot"		
Latin **terr** "land"		
Latin **scrib** "write"		
Latin **aqua** "water"		

speedometer	centimeter	manual
manufacture	erect	rectangle
pedal	pedestrian	bicycle
cyclone	vision	invisible
dictate	contradict	thermos
thermostat	territory	terrain
scribble	describe	action
react	aquarium	aquatic

Word Roots
Take It to Your Seat Centers
Reading & Language
EMC 2844 • © Evan-Moor Corp.

Word Roots
Take It to Your Seat Centers
Reading & Language
EMC 2844 • © Evan-Moor Corp.

Word Roots
Take It to Your Seat Centers
Reading & Language
EMC 2844 • © Evan-Moor Corp.

Word Roots
Take It to Your Seat Centers
Reading & Language
EMC 2844 • © Evan-Moor Corp.

Word Roots
Take It to Your Seat Centers
Reading & Language
EMC 2844 • © Evan-Moor Corp.

Word Roots
Take It to Your Seat Centers
Reading & Language
EMC 2844 • © Evan-Moor Corp.

Word Roots
Take It to Your Seat Centers
Reading & Language
EMC 2844 • © Evan-Moor Corp.

Word Roots
Take It to Your Seat Centers
Reading & Language
EMC 2844 • © Evan-Moor Corp.

Word Roots
Take It to Your Seat Centers
Reading & Language
EMC 2844 • © Evan-Moor Corp.

Word Roots
Take It to Your Seat Centers
Reading & Language
EMC 2844 • © Evan-Moor Corp.

Word Roots
Take It to Your Seat Centers
Reading & Language
EMC 2844 • © Evan-Moor Corp.

Word Roots
Take It to Your Seat Centers
Reading & Language
EMC 2844 • © Evan-Moor Corp.

Word Roots
Take It to Your Seat Centers
Reading & Language
EMC 2844 • © Evan-Moor Corp.

Word Roots
Take It to Your Seat Centers
Reading & Language
EMC 2844 • © Evan-Moor Corp.

Word Roots
Take It to Your Seat Centers
Reading & Language
EMC 2844 • © Evan-Moor Corp.

Word Roots
Take It to Your Seat Centers
Reading & Language
EMC 2844 • © Evan-Moor Corp.

Word Roots
Take It to Your Seat Centers
Reading & Language
EMC 2844 • © Evan-Moor Corp.

Word Roots
Take It to Your Seat Centers
Reading & Language
EMC 2844 • © Evan-Moor Corp.

Word Roots
Take It to Your Seat Centers
Reading & Language
EMC 2844 • © Evan-Moor Corp.

Word Roots
Take It to Your Seat Centers
Reading & Language
EMC 2844 • © Evan-Moor Corp.

Word Roots
Take It to Your Seat Centers
Reading & Language
EMC 2844 • © Evan-Moor Corp.

Word Roots
Take It to Your Seat Centers
Reading & Language
EMC 2844 • © Evan-Moor Corp.

Word Roots
Take It to Your Seat Centers
Reading & Language
EMC 2844 • © Evan-Moor Corp.

Word Roots
Take It to Your Seat Centers
Reading & Language
EMC 2844 • © Evan-Moor Corp.

Take It to Your Seat Centers

Homographs

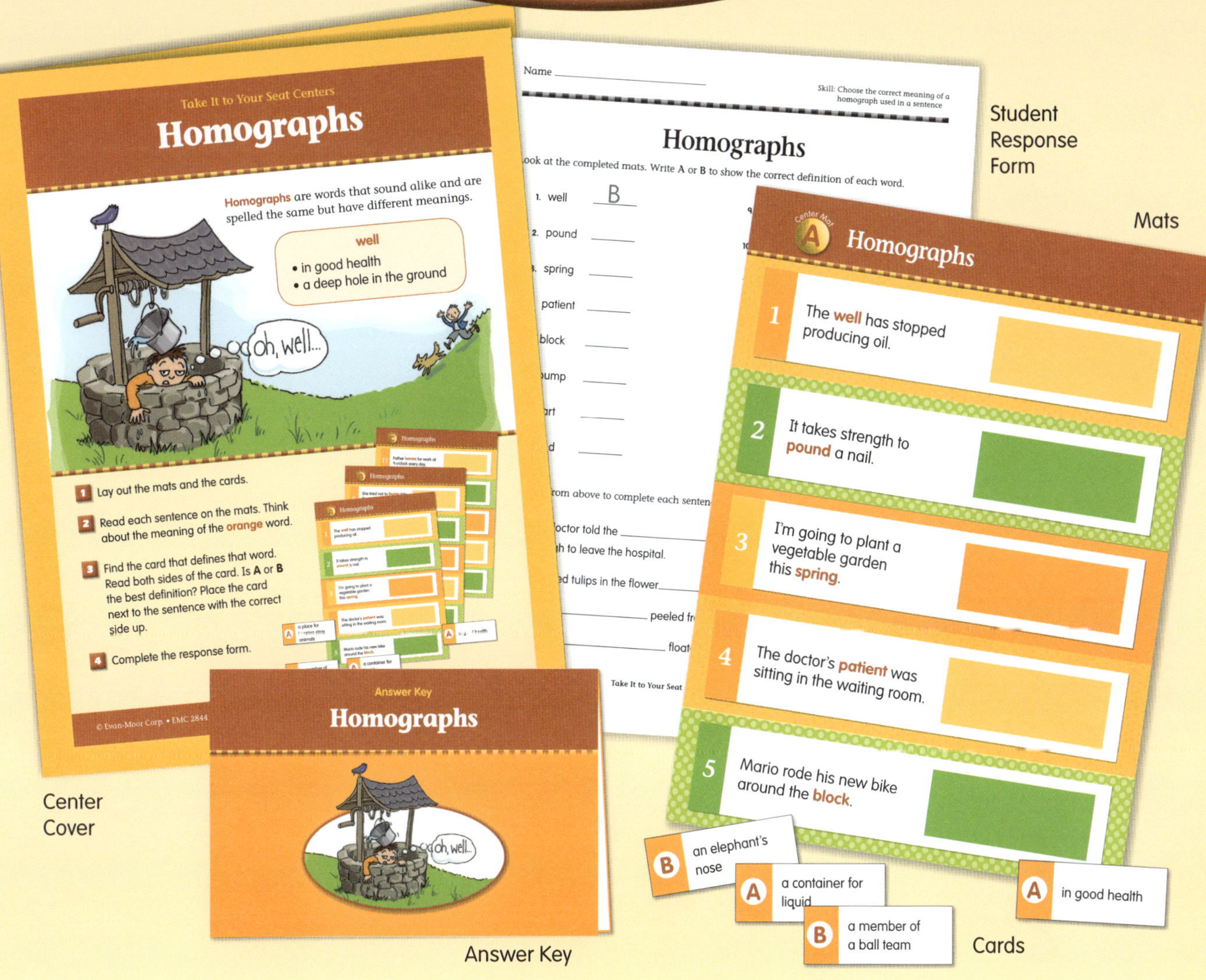

Skill

Choose the correct meaning of a homograph used in a sentence

Prepare the Center

Follow the directions on page 3.

Introduce the Center

Demonstrate how to use the center. State the goal: *You will read sentences containing a homograph, then find the matching definition card to show the meaning of each homograph.*

Name ______________________

Skill: Choose the correct meaning of a homograph used in a sentence

Homographs

Look at the completed mats. Write **A** or **B** to show the correct definition of each word.

1. well B
2. pound ____
3. spring ____
4. patient ____
5. block ____
6. bump ____
7. part ____
8. land ____
9. pitcher ____
10. trunk ____
11. leaves ____
12. watch ____
13. rock ____
14. bed ____
15. bark ____

Use words from above to complete each sentence.

1. The doctor told the ____________ that he was ____________ enough to leave the hospital.
2. I planted tulips in the flower____________ last ____________.
3. The ____________ peeled from the tree like the skin of an orange, and the ____________ floated to the ground.

Take It to Your Seat Centers

Homographs

Homographs are words that sound alike and are spelled the same but have different meanings.

well

- in good health
- a deep hole in the ground

1. Lay out the mats and the cards.
2. Read each sentence on the mats. Think about the meaning of the **orange** word.
3. Find the card that defines that word. Read both sides of the card. Is **A** or **B** the best definition? Place the card next to the sentence with the correct side up.
4. Complete the response form.

Homographs

Answer Key

(fold)

Response Form

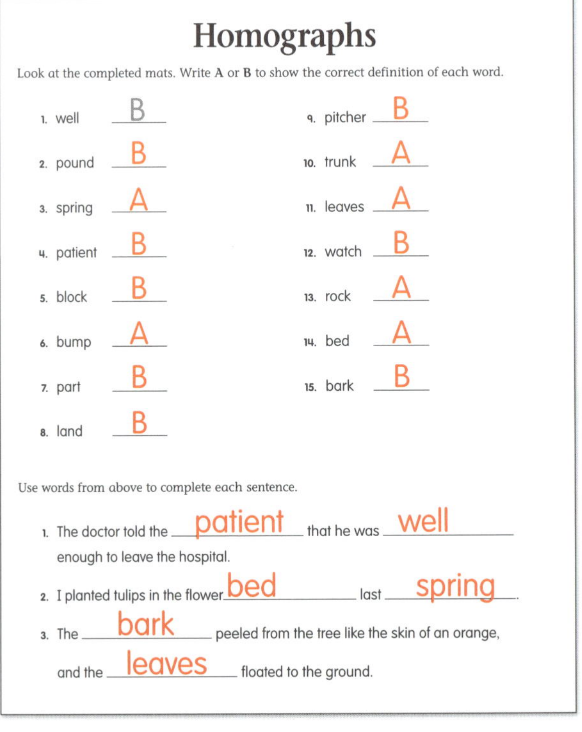

Homographs

Look at the completed mats. Write **A** or **B** to show the correct definition of each word.

1. well B
2. pound B
3. spring A
4. patient B
5. block B
6. bump A
7. part B
8. land B
9. pitcher B
10. trunk A
11. leaves A
12. watch B
13. rock A
14. bed A
15. bark B

Use words from above to complete each sentence.

1. The doctor told the patient that he was well enough to leave the hospital.
2. I planted tulips in the flower bed last spring.
3. The bark peeled from the tree like the skin of an orange, and the leaves floated to the ground.

Answer Key

Homographs

B

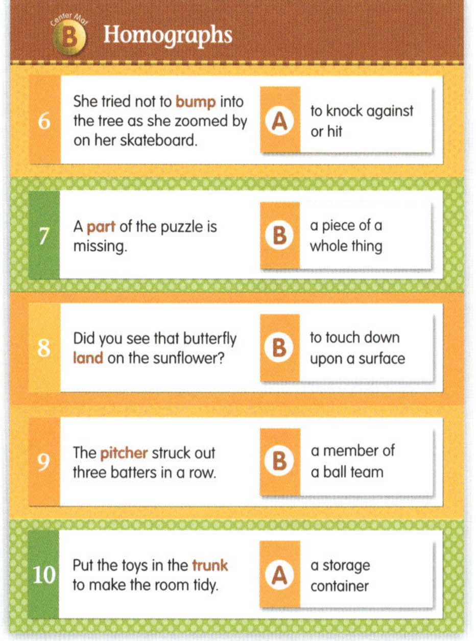

C

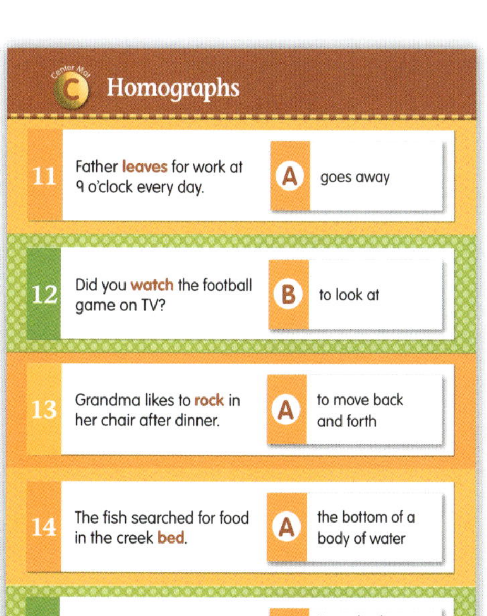

Center Mat A

Homographs

1 The **well** has stopped producing oil.

2 It takes strength to **pound** a nail.

3 I'm going to plant a vegetable garden this **spring**.

4 The doctor's **patient** was sitting in the waiting room.

5 Mario rode his new bike around the **block**.

Center Mat B

Homographs

6 She tried not to **bump** into the tree as she zoomed by on her skateboard.

7 A **part** of the puzzle is missing.

8 Did you see that butterfly **land** on the sunflower?

9 The **pitcher** struck out three batters in a row.

10 Put the toys in the **trunk** to make the room tidy.

Center Mat C

Homographs

11 Father **leaves** for work at 9 o'clock every day.

12 Did you **watch** the football game on TV?

13 Grandma likes to **rock** in her chair after dinner.

14 The fish searched for food in the creek **bed**.

15 Did you hear Spike **bark** last night?

A	in good health	A	a container for liquid
A	a place for keeping stray animals	A	a storage container
A	the season after winter	A	goes away
A	able to wait without becoming upset	A	a device for measuring time
A	a cube of hard material	A	to move back and forth
A	to knock against or hit	A	the bottom of a body of water
A	a role in a play	A	the outside cover of a tree
A	the solid part of Earth's surface		

B a member of a ball team

B an elephant's nose

B parts of a plant

B to look at

B a stone

B something to sleep on

B to make the sound a dog makes

B a deep hole in the ground

B to strike over and over with force

B to change position suddenly

B a person being treated by a doctor

B an area in a city enclosed by four streets

B a swelling or a lump

B a piece of a whole thing

B to touch down upon a surface

Take It to Your Seat Centers

Parts of Speech

Skill
Identify words as nouns, verbs, adjectives, or adverbs by their use in a sentence

Prepare the Center
Follow the directions on page 3.

Introduce the Center
Demonstrate how to use the center. State the goal: *You will read each sentence card, identify the part of speech of the bold word, and then place the card in the correct category on the mat.*

Name ____________________

Skill: Identify words as nouns, verbs, adjectives, or adverbs by their use in a sentence

Parts of Speech

Look at the completed mats. Write the bold word in each sentence in the correct category.

Nouns

squirrels

______

______

______

Verbs

______

______

______

______

Adjectives

______

______

______

______

Adverbs

______

______

______

______

Take It to Your Seat Centers

Parts of Speech

Nouns name a person, place, or thing.
Verbs tell what the subject is doing.
Adjectives describe a noun or a pronoun.
Adverbs tell how, when, or where.

The mighty lion snored loudly.

1. Lay out the mats.
2. Put the cards in a pile.
3. Read one card at a time. Look at the word in bold type. Is it a **noun**, **verb**, **adjective**, or **adverb**?
4. Place each card in the correct category on the mat.
5. Complete the response form.

Answer Key

Parts of Speech

(fold)

Response Form

Parts of Speech

Look at the completed mats. Write the bold word in each sentence in the correct category.

Nouns	Verbs	Adjectives	Adverbs
squirrels	sleep	soft	slowly
sun	won	tired	swiftly
sheep	danced	frisky	carefully
aquarium	galloped	speeding	softly

Answer Key

Parts of Speech

A Parts of Speech

Nouns name a person, place, or thing.

Birds, **squirrels**, and lizards live in the trees in our backyard.	The noontime **sun** shone brightly overhead.
How many **sheep** are in the pen?	The fish in the **aquarium** are hungry.

Adjectives describe a noun or a pronoun.

She laid her head on the **soft** pillow and quickly fell asleep.	A **tired** old man rested on the park bench.
Anney chased her **frisky** pup down the street.	The busy highway was filled with **speeding** cars.

B Parts of Speech

Verbs tell what the subject is doing.

Bats **sleep** hanging upside down in dark caves.	Carl **won** a shiny new skateboard in the contest.
Snowflakes **danced** across the sky as the wind blew.	The horse **galloped** across the grassy field.

Adverbs describe a verb. They tell how, when, or where.

She walked **slowly** into the dark room.	I skied **swiftly** down the steep hill.
Please drive **carefully**.	Father sang **softly** to the fussy baby.

Center Mat A

Parts of Speech

Nouns name a person, place, or thing.

Adjectives describe a noun or a pronoun.

RRRRRGGRRGGGR RGGRGGRGGGGG

Center Mat B

Parts of Speech

Verbs tell what the subject is doing.

Adverbs describe a verb. They tell how, when, or where.

Birds, **squirrels**, and lizards live in the trees in our backyard.	Bats **sleep** hanging upside down in dark caves.
The noontime **sun** shone brightly overhead.	Carl **won** a shiny new skateboard in the contest.
How many **sheep** are in the pen?	Snowflakes **danced** across the sky as the wind blew.
The fish in the **aquarium** are hungry.	The horse **galloped** across the grassy field.

Parts of Speech

Take It to Your Seat Centers—Reading & Language
EMC 2844 • © Evan-Moor Corp.

Parts of Speech

Take It to Your Seat Centers—Reading & Language
EMC 2844 • © Evan-Moor Corp.

Parts of Speech

Take It to Your Seat Centers—Reading & Language
EMC 2844 • © Evan-Moor Corp.

Parts of Speech

Take It to Your Seat Centers—Reading & Language
EMC 2844 • © Evan-Moor Corp.

Parts of Speech

Take It to Your Seat Centers—Reading & Language
EMC 2844 • © Evan-Moor Corp.

Parts of Speech

Take It to Your Seat Centers—Reading & Language
EMC 2844 • © Evan-Moor Corp.

Parts of Speech

Take It to Your Seat Centers—Reading & Language
EMC 2844 • © Evan-Moor Corp.

Parts of Speech

Take It to Your Seat Centers—Reading & Language
EMC 2844 • © Evan-Moor Corp.

She laid her head on the **soft** pillow and quickly fell asleep.	She walked **slowly** into the dark room.
A **tired** old man rested on the park bench.	I skied **swiftly** down the steep hill.
Anney chased her **frisky** pup down the street.	Please drive **carefully**.
The busy highway was filled with **speeding** cars.	Father sang **softly** to the fussy baby.

Parts of Speech

Take It to Your Seat Centers—Reading & Language
EMC 2844 • © Evan-Moor Corp.

Parts of Speech

Take It to Your Seat Centers—Reading & Language
EMC 2844 • © Evan-Moor Corp.

Parts of Speech

Take It to Your Seat Centers—Reading & Language
EMC 2844 • © Evan-Moor Corp.

Parts of Speech

Take It to Your Seat Centers—Reading & Language
EMC 2844 • © Evan-Moor Corp.

Parts of Speech

Take It to Your Seat Centers—Reading & Language
EMC 2844 • © Evan-Moor Corp.

Parts of Speech

Take It to Your Seat Centers—Reading & Language
EMC 2844 • © Evan-Moor Corp.

Parts of Speech

Take It to Your Seat Centers—Reading & Language
EMC 2844 • © Evan-Moor Corp.

Parts of Speech

Take It to Your Seat Centers—Reading & Language
EMC 2844 • © Evan-Moor Corp.

Take It to Your Seat Centers

Similes

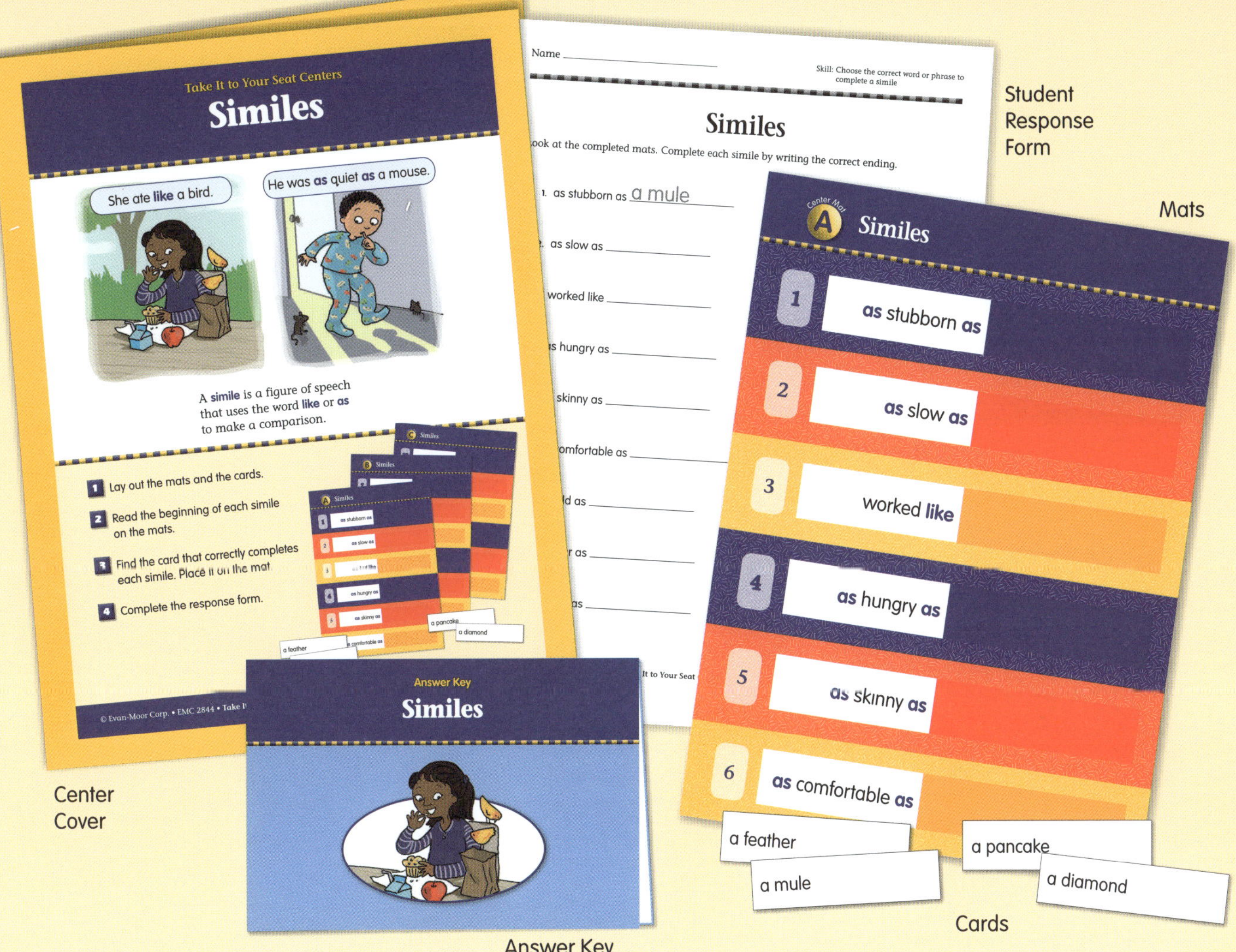

Center Cover

Student Response Form

Mats

Answer Key

Cards

Skill
Choose the correct word or phrase to complete a simile

Prepare the Center
Follow the directions on page 3.

Introduce the Center
Demonstrate how to use the center. State the goal: *You will read the beginning part of each simile, then place the card that completes it on the mat.*

Name ______________________

Skill: Choose the correct word or phrase to complete a simile

Similes

Look at the completed mats. Complete each simile by writing the correct ending.

1. as stubborn as a mule
2. as slow as ______________
3. worked like ______________
4. as hungry as ______________
5. as skinny as ______________
6. as comfortable as ______________
7. as cold as ______________
8. as clear as ______________
9. as hard as ______________
10. sparkled like ______________
11. as busy as ______________
12. waddled like ______________
13. as flat as ______________
14. as strong as ______________
15. as light as ______________
16. chattered like ______________
17. as cute as ______________
18. as sly as ______________

Take It to Your Seat Centers

Similes

A **simile** is a figure of speech that uses the word **like** or **as** to make a comparison.

1. Lay out the mats and the cards.
2. Read the beginning of each simile on the mats.
3. Find the card that correctly completes each simile. Place it on the mat.
4. Complete the response form.

Answer Key

Similes

(fold)

Response Form

Similes

Look at the completed mats. Complete each simile by writing the correct ending.

1. as stubborn as a mule
2. as slow as molasses
3. worked like a dog
4. as hungry as a bear
5. as skinny as a rail
6. as comfortable as an old shoe
7. as cold as ice
8. as clear as a bell
9. as hard as a rock
10. sparkled like a diamond
11. as busy as a bee
12. waddled like a duck
13. as flat as a pancake
14. as strong as an ox
15. as light as a feather
16. chattered like a monkey
17. as cute as a button
18. as sly as a fox

Answer Key

Similes

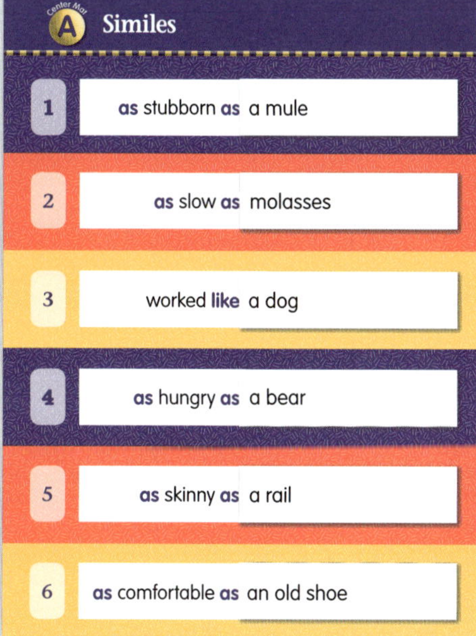

B

C

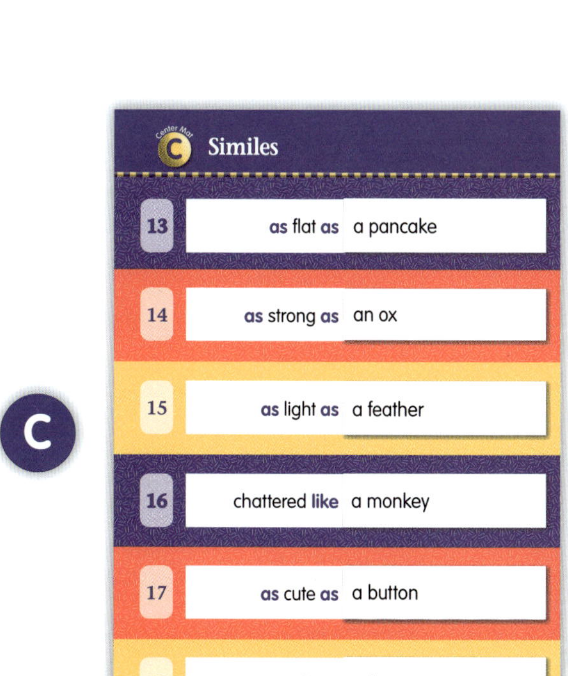

Center Mat A

Similes

1 as stubborn as

2 as slow as

3 worked like

4 as hungry as

5 as skinny as

6 as comfortable as

Center Mat B

Similes

7	**as** cold **as**
8	**as** clear **as**
9	**as** hard **as**
10	sparkled **like**
11	**as** busy **as**
12	waddled **like**

Center Mat C

Similes

13 as flat as

14 as strong as

15 as light as

16 chattered like

17 as cute as

18 as sly as

a mule	molasses
a bear	a bell
ice	a rail
a diamond	a bee
a pancake	a fox
a feather	a monkey
a dog	an old shoe
a rock	a duck
an ox	a button

Name ______________________

Skill: Identify the relationship between objects in an analogy

Analogies

Look at the completed mats. Fill in the missing part of each analogy.

1. thirsty : drink :: hungry : eat
2. clock : tick :: bell : ______________________
3. corn : vegetable :: peach : ______________________
4. happy : laugh :: sad : ______________________
5. room : house :: branch : ______________________
6. bear : den :: bee : ______________________
7. car : garage :: stove : ______________________
8. ear : hear :: nose : ______________________
9. computer : office :: tractor : ______________________
10. car : driver :: plane : ______________________
11. date : calendar :: time : ______________________
12. scales : snake :: feathers : ______________________
13. glass : break :: paper : ______________________
14. paint : artist :: guitar : ______________________
15. woman : aunt :: man : ______________________
16. paw : bear :: fin : ______________________
17. wrist : hand :: ankle : ______________________
18. shoes : feet :: gloves : ______________________

Take It to Your Seat Centers

Analogies

In an **analogy**, each pair of items has the same relationship.

bird is to **sky** as **fish** is to **sea**

Here is a shorter way to write an analogy:

bird : sky :: fish : sea

1. Lay out the mats and the cards.
2. Read each analogy on the mats. Think about how the objects are related.
3. Find the card that correctly completes the analogy and place it on the mat.
4. Complete the response form.

Answer Key

Analogies

(fold)

Response Form

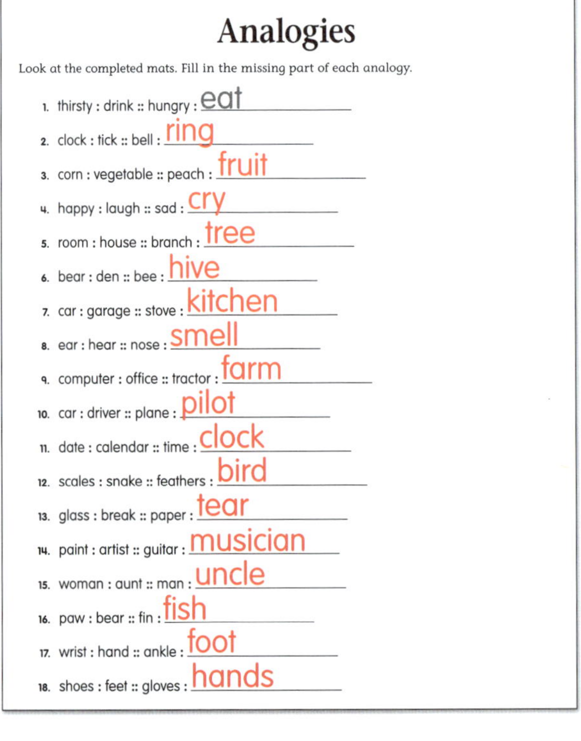

Analogies

Look at the completed mats. Fill in the missing part of each analogy.

1. thirsty : drink :: hungry : eat
2. clock : tick :: bell : ring
3. corn : vegetable :: peach : fruit
4. happy : laugh :: sad : cry
5. room : house :: branch : tree
6. bear : den :: bee : hive
7. car : garage :: stove : kitchen
8. ear : hear :: nose : smell
9. computer : office :: tractor : farm
10. car : driver :: plane : pilot
11. date : calendar :: time : clock
12. scales : snake :: feathers : bird
13. glass : break :: paper : tear
14. paint : artist :: guitar : musician
15. woman : aunt :: man : uncle
16. paw : bear :: fin : fish
17. wrist : hand :: ankle : foot
18. shoes : feet :: gloves : hands

Answer Key

Analogies

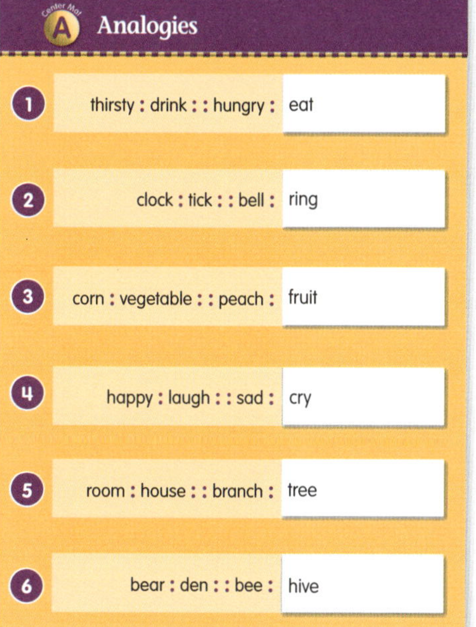

A Analogies

1. thirsty : drink : : hungry : eat
2. clock : tick : : bell : ring
3. corn : vegetable : : peach : fruit
4. happy : laugh : : sad : cry
5. room : house : : branch : tree
6. bear : den : : bee : hive

B

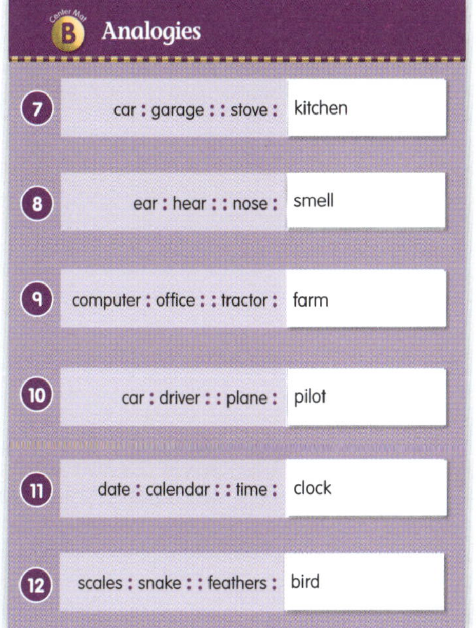

B Analogies

7. car : garage : : stove : kitchen
8. ear : hear : : nose : smell
9. computer : office : : tractor : farm
10. car : driver : : plane : pilot
11. date : calendar : : time : clock
12. scales : snake : : feathers : bird

C

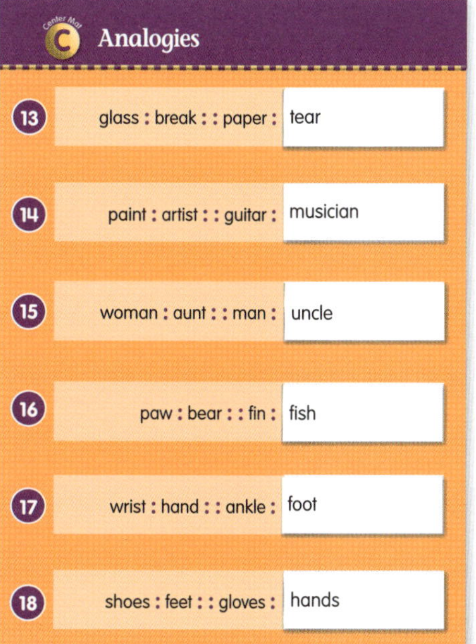

C Analogies

13. glass : break : : paper : tear
14. paint : artist : : guitar : musician
15. woman : aunt : : man : uncle
16. paw : bear : : fin : fish
17. wrist : hand : : ankle : foot
18. shoes : feet : : gloves : hands

Center Mat A

Analogies

1. thirsty : drink : : hungry :

2. clock : tick : : bell :

3. corn : vegetable : : peach :

4. happy : laugh : : sad :

5. room : house : : branch :

6. bear : den : : bee :

Center Mat B

Analogies

7 car : garage : : stove :

8 ear : hear : : nose :

9 computer : office : : tractor :

10 car : driver : : plane :

11 date : calendar : : time :

12 scales : snake : : feathers :

Center Mat C

Analogies

13 glass : break : : paper :

14 paint : artist : : guitar :

15 woman : aunt : : man :

16 paw : bear : : fin :

17 wrist : hand : : ankle :

18 shoes : feet : : gloves :

eat	cry
tree	hive
fruit	smell
musician	pilot
clock	fish
foot	tear
ring	kitchen
farm	uncle
bird	hands

Analogies

Take It to Your Seat Centers—Reading & Language
EMC 2844 • © Evan-Moor Corp.

Analogies

Take It to Your Seat Centers—Reading & Language
EMC 2844 • © Evan-Moor Corp.

Analogies

Take It to Your Seat Centers—Reading & Language
EMC 2844 • © Evan-Moor Corp.

Analogies

Take It to Your Seat Centers—Reading & Language
EMC 2844 • © Evan-Moor Corp.

Analogies

Take It to Your Seat Centers—Reading & Language
EMC 2844 • © Evan-Moor Corp.

Analogies

Take It to Your Seat Centers—Reading & Language
EMC 2844 • © Evan-Moor Corp.

Analogies

Take It to Your Seat Centers—Reading & Language
EMC 2844 • © Evan-Moor Corp.

Analogies

Take It to Your Seat Centers—Reading & Language
EMC 2844 • © Evan-Moor Corp.

Analogies

Take It to Your Seat Centers—Reading & Language
EMC 2844 • © Evan-Moor Corp.

Analogies

Take It to Your Seat Centers—Reading & Language
EMC 2844 • © Evan-Moor Corp.

Analogies

Take It to Your Seat Centers—Reading & Language
EMC 2844 • © Evan-Moor Corp.

Analogies

Take It to Your Seat Centers—Reading & Language
EMC 2844 • © Evan-Moor Corp.

Analogies

Take It to Your Seat Centers—Reading & Language
EMC 2844 • © Evan-Moor Corp.

Analogies

Take It to Your Seat Centers—Reading & Language
EMC 2844 • © Evan-Moor Corp.

Analogies

Take It to Your Seat Centers—Reading & Language
EMC 2844 • © Evan-Moor Corp.

Analogies

Take It to Your Seat Centers—Reading & Language
EMC 2844 • © Evan-Moor Corp.

Analogies

Take It to Your Seat Centers—Reading & Language
EMC 2844 • © Evan-Moor Corp.

Analogies

Take It to Your Seat Centers—Reading & Language
EMC 2844 • © Evan-Moor Corp.

Take It to Your Seat Centers

Main Idea and Details

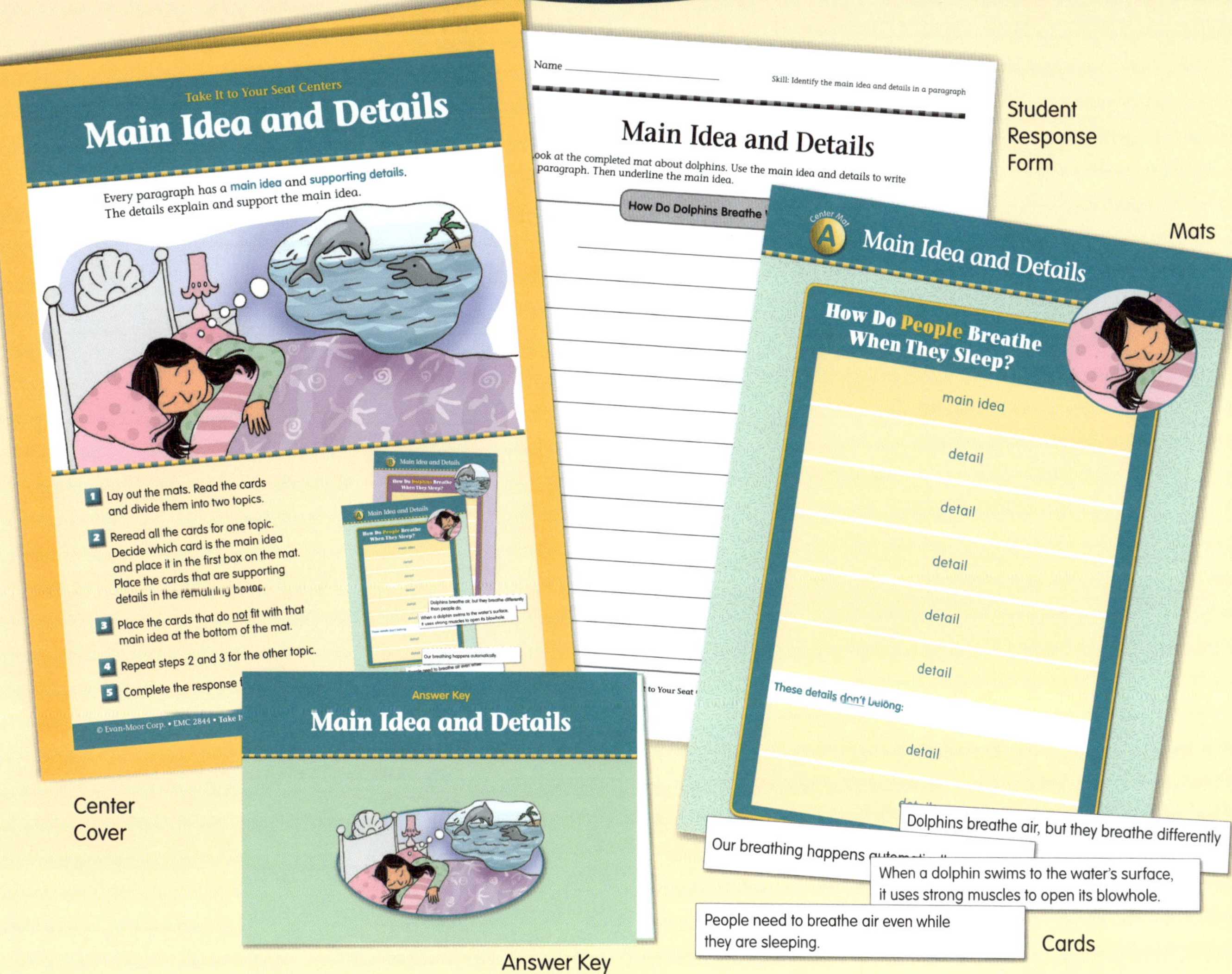

Skill
Identify the main idea and details in a paragraph

Prepare the Center
Follow the directions on page 3.

Introduce the Center
Demonstrate how to use the center. State the goal: *You will identify the main idea and details that belong and do not belong with two topics.*

Response Form

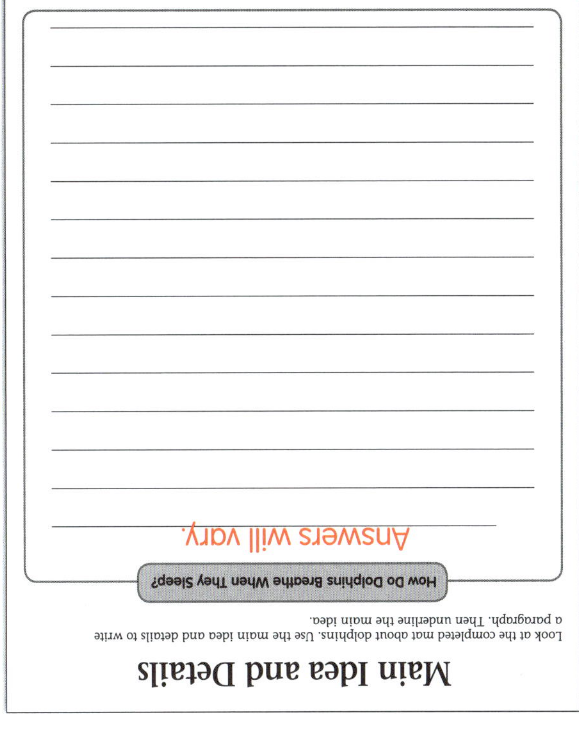
Main Idea and Details

Look at the completed mat about dolphins. Use the main idea and details to write a paragraph. Then underline the main idea.

How Do Dolphins Breathe When They Sleep?

Answers will vary.

(fold)

Answer Key

Main Idea and Details

Answer Key

Main Idea and Details

A

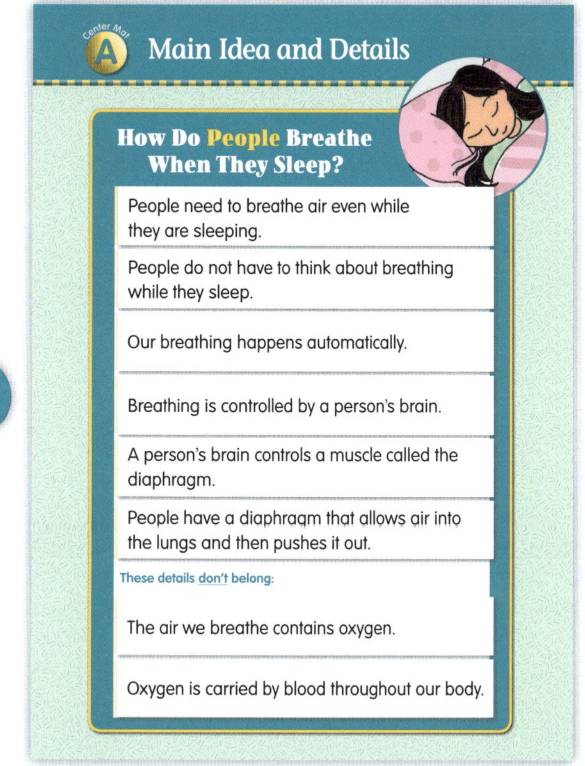

Center Mat A — Main Idea and Details

How Do People Breathe When They Sleep?

- People need to breathe air even while they are sleeping.
- People do not have to think about breathing while they sleep.
- Our breathing happens automatically.
- Breathing is controlled by a person's brain.
- A person's brain controls a muscle called the diaphragm.
- People have a diaphragm that allows air into the lungs and then pushes it out.

These details don't belong:

- The air we breathe contains oxygen.
- Oxygen is carried by blood throughout our body.

B

Center Mat B — Main Idea and Details

How Do Dolphins Breathe When They Sleep?

- Dolphins breathe air, but they breathe differently than people do.
- Dolphins breathe through a blowhole in the top of their head.
- When a dolphin swims to the water's surface, it uses strong muscles to open its blowhole.
- A dolphin must be awake to control its blowhole.
- Only half of the dolphin's brain sleeps at a time.
- The other half of its brain stays alert to help the dolphin breathe and to watch for danger.

These details don't belong:

- Dolphins live together in groups called pods.
- Dolphins sometimes help an injured dolphin get to the surface to breathe.

Main Idea and Details

How Do **People** Breathe When They Sleep?

main idea

detail

detail

detail

detail

detail

These details don't belong:

detail

detail

Center Mat B

Main Idea and Details

How Do Dolphins Breathe When They Sleep?

main idea

detail

detail

detail

detail

detail

These details don't belong:

detail

detail

People need to breathe air even while they are sleeping.

People do not have to think about breathing while they sleep.

Our breathing happens automatically.

Breathing is controlled by a person's brain.

A person's brain controls a muscle called the diaphragm.

People have a diaphragm that allows air into the lungs and then pushes it out.

The air we breathe contains oxygen.

Oxygen is carried by blood throughout our body.

Main Idea and Details

Take It to Your Seat Centers—Reading & Language

Main Idea and Details

Take It to Your Seat Centers—Reading & Language
EMC 2844 • © Evan-Moor Corp.

Main Idea and Details

Take It to Your Seat Centers—Reading & Language
EMC 2844 • © Evan-Moor Corp.

Main Idea and Details

Take It to Your Seat Centers—Reading & Language
EMC 2844 • © Evan-Moor Corp.

Main Idea and Details

Take It to Your Seat Centers—Reading & Language
EMC 2844 • © Evan-Moor Corp.

Main Idea and Details

Take It to Your Seat Centers—Reading & Language
EMC 2844 • © Evan-Moor Corp.

Main Idea and Details

Take It to Your Seat Centers—Reading & Language
EMC 2844 • © Evan-Moor Corp.

Main Idea and Details

Take It to Your Seat Centers—Reading & Language
EMC 2844 • © Evan-Moor Corp.

Dolphins breathe air, but they breathe differently than people do.
Dolphins breathe through a blowhole in the top of their head.
When a dolphin swims to the water's surface, it uses strong muscles to open its blowhole.
A dolphin must be awake to control its blowhole.
Only half of the dolphin's brain sleeps at a time.
The other half of its brain stays alert to help the dolphin breathe and to watch for danger.
Dolphins live together in groups called pods.
Dolphins sometimes help an injured dolphin get to the surface to breathe.

Main Idea and Details

Take It to Your Seat Centers—Reading & Language

Main Idea and Details

Take It to Your Seat Centers—Reading & Language
EMC 2844 • © Evan-Moor Corp.

Main Idea and Details

Take It to Your Seat Centers—Reading & Language
EMC 2844 • © Evan-Moor Corp.

Main Idea and Details

Take It to Your Seat Centers—Reading & Language
EMC 2844 • © Evan-Moor Corp.

Main Idea and Details

Take It to Your Seat Centers—Reading & Language
EMC 2844 • © Evan-Moor Corp.

Main Idea and Details

Take It to Your Seat Centers—Reading & Language
EMC 2844 • © Evan-Moor Corp.

Main Idea and Details

Take It to Your Seat Centers—Reading & Language
EMC 2844 • © Evan-Moor Corp.

Main Idea and Details

Take It to Your Seat Centers—Reading & Language
EMC 2844 • © Evan-Moor Corp.

Take It to Your Seat Centers

Fact or Opinion?

Skill
Distinguish between fact and opinion in text

Prepare the Center
Follow the directions on page 3.

Introduce the Center
Demonstrate how to use the center. State the goal: *You will separate sentences on the topic of baseball into two paragraphs—one that is factual and one that is opinion.*

Name ____________________

Fact or Opinion?

Look at the completed mats. Write the number of each card in the correct box.

Fact	Opinion
______	2
______	______
______	______
______	______
______	______
______	______
______	______
______	______

Write one fact and one opinion on the topic of **baseball**.

Fact ____________________

____

____

Opinion ____________________

____

____

Take It to Your Seat Centers

Fact or Opinion?

When you are reading, it is important to determine the difference between **fact** and **opinion**.

1. Lay out the mats and the cards. Use the cards to make two stories about baseball. One story will be full of facts and the other will be full of opinions.
2. Read each card and think about what it says. Is it a **fact** or an **opinion**?
3. Place the cards on the correct mats in order.
4. Complete the response form.

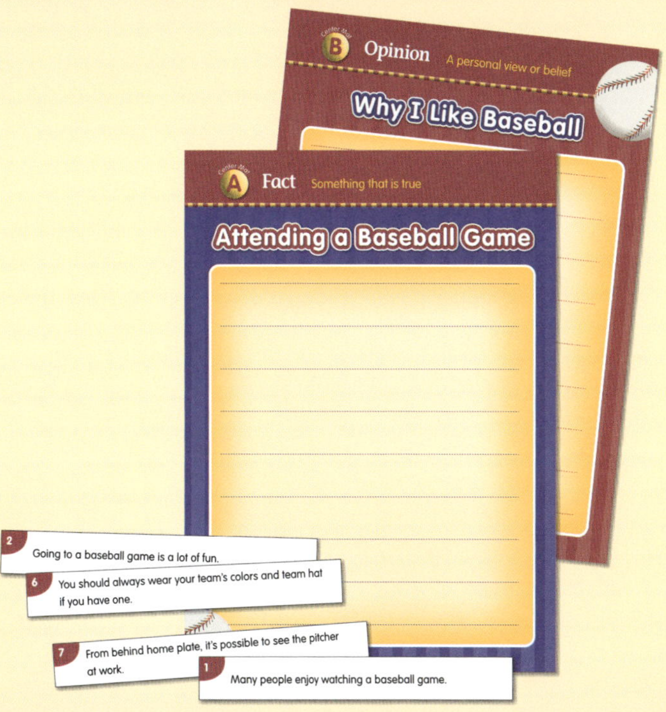

Answer Key

Fact or Opinion?

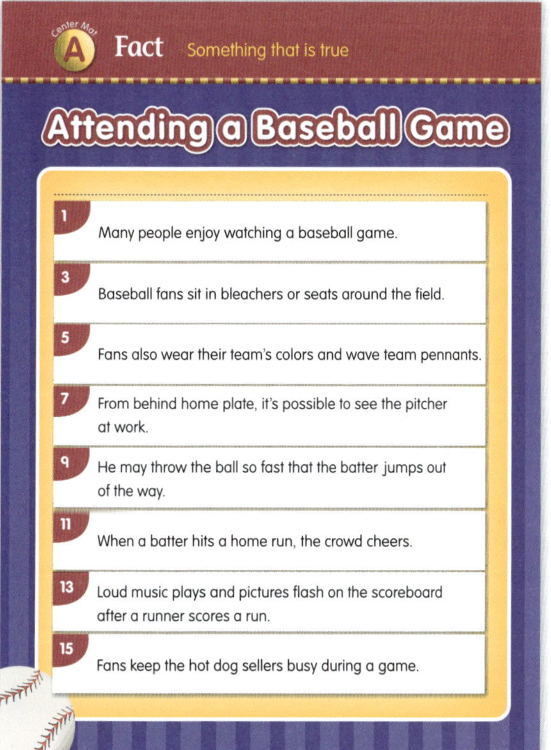

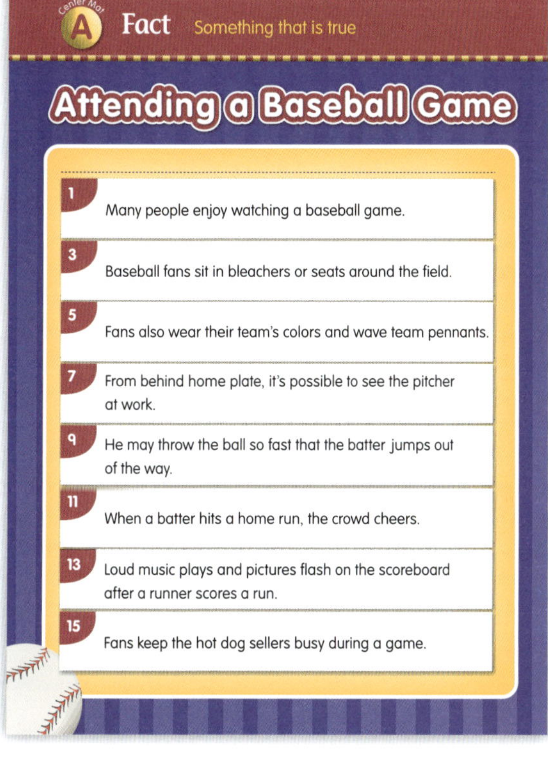

Center Mat A **Fact** Something that is true

Attending a Baseball Game

1. Many people enjoy watching a baseball game.
3. Baseball fans sit in bleachers or seats around the field.
5. Fans also wear their team's colors and wave team pennants.
7. From behind home plate, it's possible to see the pitcher at work.
9. He may throw the ball so fast that the batter jumps out of the way.
11. When a batter hits a home run, the crowd cheers.
13. Loud music plays and pictures flash on the scoreboard after a runner scores a run.
15. Fans keep the hot dog sellers busy during a game.

Center Mat B **Opinion** A personal view or belief

Why I Like Baseball

2. Going to a baseball game is a lot of fun.
4. It's best to watch the game from directly behind home plate.
6. You should always wear your team's colors and team hat if you have one.
8. The pitcher is the most interesting player to watch.
10. It's very cool when he throws a fast pitch, and the batter has to jump out of the way.
12. When a batter hits a home run, you'll be so excited that you'll be up on your feet and yelling.
14. The game gets boring if nobody hits a home run.
16. But if you enjoy a tasty hot dog, you'll be glad you came.

Center Mat A

Fact Something that is true

Attending a Baseball Game

Center Mat B

Opinion

A personal view or belief

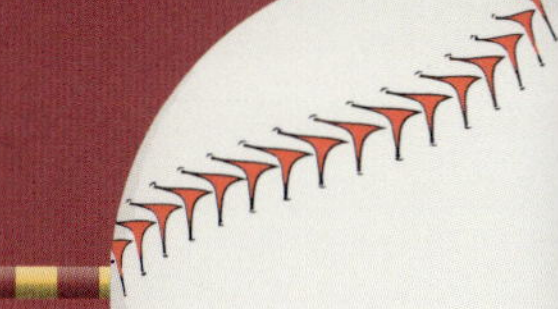

Why I Like Baseball

2	Going to a baseball game is a lot of fun.
4	It's best to watch the game from directly behind home plate.
6	You should always wear your team's colors and team hat if you have one.
8	The pitcher is the most interesting player to watch.
10	It's very cool when he throws a fast pitch, and the batter has to jump out of the way.
12	When a batter hits a home run, you'll be so excited that you'll be up on your feet and yelling.
14	The game gets boring if nobody hits a home run.
16	But if you enjoy a tasty hot dog, you'll be glad you came.

Fact or Opinion?

Take It to Your Seat Centers—Reading & Language
EMC 2844 • © Evan-Moor Corp.

Fact or Opinion?

Take It to Your Seat Centers—Reading & Language
EMC 2844 • © Evan-Moor Corp.

Fact or Opinion?

Take It to Your Seat Centers—Reading & Language
EMC 2844 • © Evan-Moor Corp.

Fact or Opinion?

Take It to Your Seat Centers—Reading & Language
EMC 2844 • © Evan-Moor Corp.

Fact or Opinion?

Take It to Your Seat Centers—Reading & Language
EMC 2844 • © Evan-Moor Corp.

Fact or Opinion?

Take It to Your Seat Centers—Reading & Language
EMC 2844 • © Evan-Moor Corp.

Fact or Opinion?

Take It to Your Seat Centers—Reading & Language
EMC 2844 • © Evan-Moor Corp.

Fact or Opinion?

Take It to Your Seat Centers—Reading & Language
EMC 2844 • © Evan-Moor Corp.

1 Many people enjoy watching a baseball game.

3 Baseball fans sit in bleachers or seats around the field.

5 Fans also wear their team's colors and wave team pennants.

7 From behind home plate, it's possible to see the pitcher at work.

9 He may throw the ball so fast that the batter jumps out of the way.

11 When a batter hits a home run, the crowd cheers.

13 Loud music plays and pictures flash on the scoreboard after a runner scores a run.

15 Fans keep the hot dog sellers busy during a game.

Fact or Opinion?
Take It to Your Seat Centers—Reading & Language
EMC 2844 • © Evan-Moor Corp.

Fact or Opinion?
Take It to Your Seat Centers—Reading & Language
EMC 2844 • © Evan-Moor Corp.

Fact or Opinion?
Take It to Your Seat Centers—Reading & Language
EMC 2844 • © Evan-Moor Corp.

Fact or Opinion?
Take It to Your Seat Centers—Reading & Language
EMC 2844 • © Evan-Moor Corp.

Fact or Opinion?
Take It to Your Seat Centers—Reading & Language
EMC 2844 • © Evan-Moor Corp.

Fact or Opinion?
Take It to Your Seat Centers—Reading & Language
EMC 2844 • © Evan-Moor Corp.

Fact or Opinion?
Take It to Your Seat Centers—Reading & Language
EMC 2844 • © Evan-Moor Corp.

Fact or Opinion?
Take It to Your Seat Centers—Reading & Language
EMC 2844 • © Evan-Moor Corp.